HISTORIES OF THE MUSICAL

Histories of the Musical

An Oxford Handbook of the American Musical, Volume 1

EDITED BY RAYMOND KNAPP

MITCHELL MORRIS

AND STACY WOLF

OXFORD
UNIVERSITY PRESS

OXFORD
UNIVERSITY PRESS

Oxford University Press is a department of the University of Oxford. It furthers
the University's objective of excellence in research, scholarship, and education
by publishing worldwide. Oxford is a registered trade mark of Oxford University
Press in the UK and certain other countries.

Published in the United States of America by Oxford University Press
198 Madison Avenue, New York, NY 10016, United States of America.

Library of Congress Cataloging-in-Publication Data
Names: Knapp, Raymond. | Morris, Mitchell, 1961– | Wolf, Stacy Ellen.
Title: Histories of the musical : an Oxford handbook of the American musical,
Volume 1 / edited by Raymond Knapp, Mitchell Morris, and Stacy Wolf.
Description: New York, NY : Oxford University Press, 2018. |
Series: Oxford handbooks | Includes bibliographical references and index.
Identifiers: LCCN 2018022217 | ISBN 9780190877767 (pbk. : alk. paper) |
ISBN 9780190877781 (epub)
Subjects: LCSH: Musicals—United States—History and criticism.
Classification: LCC ML1711 .H45 2018 | DDC 782.1/40973—dc23
LC record available at https://lccn.loc.gov/2018022217

1 3 5 7 9 8 6 4 2

Printed by WebCom, Inc., Canada

CONTENTS

CONTRIBUTORS

Geoffrey Block, Distinguished Professor Emeritus of Music History, University of Puget Sound

Liza Gennaro, professional choreographer and Assistant Professor and Head of Musical Theatre, Indiana University Department of Theatre, Drama, and Contemporary Dance

Raymond Knapp, Distinguished Professor of Musicology and Humanities, Academic Associate Dean of the Herb Alpert School of Music, and Director of the Center for Musical Humanities, University of California, Los Angeles

Paul R. Laird, Professor of Musicology, Director of the Division of Musicology, University of Kansas

Jim Lovensheimer, Associate Professor of Musicology, Vanderbilt University

Mitchell Morris, Professor of Musicology and Humanities, University of California, Los Angeles

Thomas L. Riis, Joseph and Rebecca Negler Endowed Professor of Music and Director of the American Music Research Center, University of Colorado, Boulder

Jessica Sternfeld, Associate Professor of Music History, Chapman University

Stacy Wolf, Professor of Theater and Director of the Program in Music Theater, Princeton University

Elizabeth L. Wollman, Associate Professor of Music, Baruch College and the Graduate Center, City University of New York

ABOUT THE COMPANION WEBSITE

www.oup.com/us/hotm

Oxford has created a website to accompany *The Oxford Handbook of the American Musical*, which includes nearly two hundred audio, video, image, or text examples to illustrate or augment the discussions advanced in the text. To make this valuable resource easy to use, each example is keyed to its appropriate place in the text, and numbered sequentially within each of the essays that use this resource. For clarity, we've used the following notation (these particular indications would refer to examples 5-8 in the first essay):

🔊 Example 1.5 (Audio Example 1.5)

▶ Example 1.6 (Video Example 1.6)

🖼 Example 1.7 (Image Example 1.7)

📄 Example 1.8 (Text Example 1.8)

To access an example, simply click on the appropriate icon on the website.

HISTORIES OF THE MUSICAL

Introduction

THE AMERICAN MUSICAL IS A paradox. On stage or screen, musicals at once hold a dominant and a contested place in the worlds of entertainment, art, and scholarship. Born from a mélange of performance forms that included opera and operetta, vaudeville and burlesque, minstrelsy and jazz, musicals have always sought to amuse more than instruct, and to make money more than make political change. In spite of their unapologetic commercialism, though, musicals have achieved supreme artistry and have influenced culture as much as if not more than any other art form in America, including avantgarde and high art on the one hand, and the full range of popular and commercial art on the other. Reflecting, refracting, and shaping U.S. culture since the early twentieth century, musicals converse with shifting dynamics of gender and sexuality, ethnicity and race, and the very question of what it means to be American and to be human. The musical explores identity, self-determination, and the American dream.

The form of the musical—the combination of music, dance, speech, and design—is paradoxical, too. By the middle of the twentieth century, spoken scenes in musicals were expected to conform to the style of nonmusical plays, with characters psychologized and realistically portrayed. When characters burst into song or dance, a different expressive mode took over, one that scholars like Richard Dyer have seen as utopian.[1] Even as artists aimed for "integration" among the musical's disparate parts, in emulation of Wagner's "total artwork," the pieces required different skills of creation, presentation, and interpretation. As Scott McMillin argues in *The Musical as Drama*, "When a musical is working well, I feel the crackle of difference... between the book and the numbers, between songs and dances, between dance and spoken dialogue."[2] In part because of its hybrid form and its commercial aspirations, the musical failed to register as a legitimate topic for scholarly study in either music or theater programs in universities until near the end of the twentieth century. Although audiences flocked to see *The Phantom of the Opera* on Broadway to the tune of 140 million people (as of 2017) worldwide since its opening year on Broadway (1987), and the film of *The Sound of Music* (1965) held its place as the most popular movie musical of all time well into the twenty-first century, few college courses taught the history or criticism of musicals. And while young composers, lyricists, librettists, designers, and performers honed their craft and enrolled in professional training programs, they gained knowledge of the musical's history and theory through practice rather than through college classes that emphasized a scholarly approach to musicals.

Beginning in the 1990s, and gaining considerable momentum across the first decade(s) of the new millennium, the study of American musicals on stage and on film has grown rapidly into a legitimate field. Many universities now offer surveys of musical theater or film history; or build a course focused on a composer, a subgenre, or a period in U.S. history; or include musicals in other courses, from American drama to popular culture to African American studies.[3] In departments of music and musicology, theater, film, media studies, and literature, more courses are taught each year about musicals or include the study of a musical play or film as an example of cultural or performance history. Increasingly, musical theater, musical films, and musicals in other media, such as television or online, are seen as viable objects of scholarly inquiry.

Scholarship to support the study of musicals is gradually catching up to the enthusiastic reception of students, as more dissertations are written and books published on musicals each year. Where there were formerly only encyclopedic lists of musicals and their creators, coffee-table tomes, or hagiographies, there is now a growing field of academic studies of musicals. Some explicate and analyze a range of musicals; others trace a chronological history. Some authors stress context over analysis, locating musicals historically, and some books consider musicals from specific identity positions. Increasingly, studies focus on a single musical, often relying on archival research to unearth details about the production process. Finally, books take a biographical approach and center on a director, composer, choreographer, producer, performer, or another member of the creative team.

Even as scholarship has grown in diverse and wide-ranging ways, the teaching of musicals continues to be extremely challenging. This book, in its original one-volume edition, grew out of our mutual passion for teaching musicals and our mutual frustration with available pedagogically oriented materials. When the three of us first met to talk about musicals, we complained—as most professors do—about the lack of a textbook for teaching musicals that adequately covered the wide range of possible approaches to the subject. Each of us had solved the problem in our own way, using a combination of texts and articles and our own expertise. From that start, we found common goals as instructors: first, to situate the musical historically; second, to locate the ideological work of the musical as "American"; and third, to practice a variety of methods and techniques to analyze musicals. Moreover, each of us was well aware of the strengths and weaknesses in our training, of the stubborn disciplinarity of each of our fields, and of the tendency to privilege one element of the musical over another based on our comfort level. We knew that a useful textbook for the study of the American musical needed more than our three voices to write it.

Although we designed our book as a teaching tool, we mean "teaching" in the broadest possible way for students, instructors, and the general reader. We intended our book not (necessarily) to be read cover to cover, nor (necessarily) assigned in order, but as a resource for instructors, students, and aficionados of the musical and as a complement to other studies currently available. As well, scholars expert in one area of the musical might use our book as a first resource in coming to terms with other aspects of the art form less familiar to them and as an additional resource for courses on related topics, such as Tin Pan Alley or Popular Song.

Since the publication of *The Oxford Handbook of the American Musical* in 2011, the American musical continues to thrive, both reflecting and shaping cultural values and social norms, and even commenting on politics, whether directly and on a national scale (*Hamilton* [2015]) or somewhat more obliquely and on a more intimate scale (*Fun Home* [2015]). New stage musicals, such as *Come from Away* (2017) and *The Band's Visit* (2017), open on Broadway every season, challenging conventions of form and content, and revivals offer audiences a different perspective on extant shows (*Carousel* [2018]; *My Fair Lady* [2018]). Television musicals broadcast live, including *Peter Pan Live!* (2014) and *The Wiz Live!* (2015), at once hearken back to 1950s television's affection for musical theatre and aim to attract new audiences through the accessibility of television. Film musicals, including *Les Misérables* (2012) and *Into the Woods* (2014), capitalize on the medium's technical capabilities of perspective and point of view, as well as visual spectacle. Television has embraced the genre anew, and with unexpected gusto, not only devising musical episodes for countless dramatic and comedy series, but also generating musical series such as *Galavant* (2015-16) and *Crazy Ex-Girlfriend* (2015-).

And animated musicals, such as Disney's *Moana* (2016), hail child and adult audiences with their dual messages, vibrant visual vocabulary, and hummable music.

The essays gathered in this book, Volume I of the reissued *Oxford Handbook*, are written by leading scholars in the field, and explore the American musical from both the outside and the inside. This first volume concentrates in particular on large-scale, more philosophical issues of relevance to the genre, considering issues of historical situations and formal procedure as they bear on the narratives we make concerning productions and performers, artists and audiences, commerce and context. The first four essays discuss ways of defining histories and texts, and apprehending the formal choices of singers and dancers; the second group of four take up the subtle challenges of the genre's signal transformations out of minstrelsy and Tin Pan Alley to "integration" and beyond.

For much of the genre's history, telling the story of the American musical was also tacitly a way of telling a story about American politics and society. It matters that the musical as it is commonly understood emerged from a complex of popular entertainments that it constantly gestured back towards. This book approaches the entanglements of performance and society in two acts.

The first two chapters consider fundamental issues of making history. What kinds of decisions do we make about the narratives we tell, whether they are tales of Golden Ages past or revolutions newly commenced? And how do we decide on the people and things to discuss in the first place? Given the richly collaborative, decentered nature of the American musical, how do we establish those islands of narrative stability we call authors and texts? Both chapters are concerned with making things specific; by contrast, the following two chapters, on musical styles and conventions and on the place of dance in the "Golden Age," look outward to the matrix of song and movement circulating in American culture more broadly during the Twentieth Century. A musical, as a text embedded in its own history, is also a site in which multiple currents of sound and movement are sedimented in the content.

That process is one of sedimentation, in which older historical styles and significances return in multiple guises: as tributes, as parodies, as stylizations, as abstractions, as gestural ghosts. A deep history of the genre must take account of crucial phases of American cultural history and acknowledge the creative and painful work of minstrelsy. The complex of domination and fantasy that underwrote minstrel performance created the "miscegenated," adroitly hybrid musical styles that found their way into the welter of ethnicities that populated urban centers at the turn of the last century—and nowhere more vividly than New York City, where the commerce of Tin Pan Alley built itself out of minstrel song in particular. Reflections on this history are the concern of the fifth and sixth essays in this volume, as they draw attention to the genre's grounding. The final two chapters of this volume address the most familiar historical constructs found in narratives on the American musical: the notion of "Integration," and the accompanying vision of Broadway's "Golden Age." Both terms have been idolized in ways that bring them in for the well-earned critiques of these essays; but as the authors also demonstrate, the terms continue to have potent uses, and their power speaks to broader issues of aesthetic, social, and moral concern.

Whatever its media or format, and however its histories are told, the musical is perhaps the most intricately collaborative art and entertainment form in US culture. When audiences experience the emotional tug and infectious energy of a musical, they might not perceive the work of the many practitioners who contribute to the final production, nor the histories and conventions that underwrite and inflect their work, deepening the collaborative process to include earlier practitioners. The work of artists for the musical not only relies on their own areas of expertise, but also requires that they participate in art-making with others, each following or departing from separate if intertwined lineages and speaking different artistic languages. Artists who enjoy making musicals appreciate the give and take of collaboration. As the great composer and lyricist Stephen Sondheim told Hamilton creator Lin-Manuel Miranda, "Well, I collaborate with people. My spark often comes from collaborators. . . . I mean, I'm a collaborative animal. . . . I need the spur. And the spur and the boost comes [sic] from somebody else, generally."[4]

Mitchell Morris

ACKNOWLEDGMENTS

Any book this complex—like the musical itself—has innumerable contributors beyond those headlined as editors and authors. The editors are extremely grateful for the abundant and varied support their scholarly communities have provided. On the institutional level, this included support, at UCLA, from the Office of Instructional Development, the Department of Musicology, and the Council on Research, along with a rich field of interactions among students and other faculty; we are especially grateful for insights that have found their way into this book from Juliana Gondek, Peter Kazaras, Elijah Wald, Sam Baltimore, Sarah Ellis, and Holley Replogle-Wong, and for Holley's exemplary work preparing and organizing materials for the book's Web site. At Princeton, we thank the Lewis Center for the Arts, especially Chair Michael Cadden. We thank Senior Production Editor Joellyn Ausanka for guiding us through the copyediting and proofing stages of the book. Norm Hirschy at Oxford

University Press has been unfailingly, even brilliantly helpful, at every step of the process. And, for the reissued volumes, we have been blessed with the guidance, expertise, and patience of Lauralee Yeary.

Raymond Knapp, Mitchell Morris, Stacy Wolf

NOTES

1. Richard Dyer, "Entertainment and Utopia," in *Genre: The Musical*, ed. Rick Altman (London: Routledge and Kegan Paul, 1981); originally published in *Movie* 2 [Spring 1977]: 2–13).
2. Scott McMillin, *The Musical as Drama: A Study of the Principles and Conventions behind Musical Shows from Kern to Sondheim* (Princeton: Princeton University Press, 2006), p. 2.
3. See Stacy Wolf, "In Defense of Pleasure: Musical Theatre History in the Liberal Arts [A Manifesto]," *Theatre Topics* 17.1 (March 2007): 51–60.
4. Lin-Manuel Miranda, "Stephen Sondheim, Theater's Greatest Lyricist," *New York Times*, October 16, 2017. https://www.nytimes.com/2017/10/16/t-magazine/lin-manuel-miranda-stephen-sondheim.html?_r=0 Accessed November 25, 2017.

PART ONE

HISTORIOGRAPHY

1

Narratives and Values

MITCHELL MORRIS

■ □ ■

It warms my heart to know that you/Remember still the way you do.
—MADAME ALVAREZ, *Gigi*

STUDIES OF THE MUSICAL AS a genre, as well as its precursors, spin-offs, and assorted cousins, typically shape themselves as accounts of change over time. To some extent, this is inherent in any popular genre of the arts: contemporaneity and fashionability are powerful values, and they gain their effectiveness only by contrast, explicit or implicit, with what came before them. The matrix of commercial necessities that enable the musical has therefore tended to foreground notions of "the new." As a sense of "tradition" has developed among artists and audiences, the notion of "the revival" has also become increasingly vivid. Attributes such as these indicate a general assumption that the historical location of a musical— not simply its place in the chronological sequence, but also the networks of affiliation and disaffiliation to other works in that sequence—is an important aspect of its framing. That location contributes to the set of expectations that we bring to the experience as audiences and artists (not only of revivals, but also of works that play on the forms and contents of the past). It also enables the construction of accounts of the musical as a genre that exists through time. We usually call such accounts "history." But what exactly do we mean when we call something "history"? And more specifically, what problems must we consider when we think about writing or reading the history of the musical? This chapter briefly explores these questions.

MAKING HISTORY

The oldest extant forms that record change through time are usually called "chronicles." The *Oxford English Dictionary* gives its first definition of this term as "a detailed and continuous register of events in order of time; a historical record, *esp.* one in which the facts are narrated without philosophic treatment, or any attempt at literary style."[1] This is not to say that the events registered are completely random—chronicles normally focus on relatively specific subject matter, whether it be lists of kings or presidents, meteorological or astronomical conditions, or performances of dramatic or musical works. What matters here is that chronicles are in some sense "pre-reflective," that is, they are primarily oriented toward listing events, not explaining them, and there is probably no overt reflection on the writer's selection of entries; the criterion for an event's inclusion in a chronicle is typically its membership in the class of events the chronicle aims to document. Chronicles exist from the earliest periods of written records and continue in various forms to the present day, no doubt because temporal ordering is typically central to the ways human life tends to be lived. All languages, after all, have ways of indicating past, present, and future.

History, by contrast, departs from the list of events in time by seeking various kinds of causal connections. That is, histories construct narratives of one sort or another; the events or series of events are linked in speech or writing to form a chain of causal relationships that may be roughly simultaneous (synchronic) and/or spread out over time (diachronic). The word "history" itself comes from the fifth century bce Greek writer Herodotus of Halicarnassus, who called his account of the origins of the Greek and Persian wars an "inquiry" or *historía*.[2] History seeks to answer questions such as how or why events have occurred, how or why events are related.

Fundamental to the construction of a specifically historical narrative is reliance on forms of documentation: oral histories and folk tales or myths, eyewitness accounts of events, artifacts (typically the place where history begins to merge with archaeology), and written documents of many types. Such documents may be cited without question, especially in earlier historical accounts, but more often a historian spends considerable time reading the documents critically. In what context was a given document created, and what was it to be used for? Given the marked tendency of memories to undergo modification over time and the common human tendency to favor some interests above others, to what degree can a given document be trusted as an impartial account? When two or more documents disagree, how can they be evaluated, and how do we choose between the versions of an event that they offer? Historians characteristically aspire to factual accuracy, and critical assessment is a crucial part of a historian's task. A history is different from a fictional account precisely because it attempts to base its narrative on facts. But this then raises the question of defining the term "fact."

For the purposes of this discussion, a fact may be defined as a falsifiable propositional statement about an event, a person, an object, and so on. An example: "The original Broadway production of Rodgers and Hammerstein's *Oklahoma!* opened on March 31, 1943." This statement seems unassailable because there are so many bits of documentary evidence—newspaper reviews, paylists for musicians or stage crew, first-person recollections, and the other written materials accumulated around the production—that agree in supporting it. The process of falsification would depend on assembling supporting evidence—in this understanding of historical research, almost certainly documents of some sort—to support the new claim. The process of evaluating and deciding between these contradictory documents would be a central task for writing history.

So far this seems sensible, indeed unremarkable. But consider what is presupposed in the statement. The musical is specified as the work of a composer-lyricist team; other collaborators such as Agnes de Mille (choreographer), Lemuel Ayers (scenic designer), or Rouben Mamoulian (director) are left unmentioned. This choice is in keeping with our assumption that music and text are the stable components of a musical, and the other elements of the production more-or-less variable— assumptions that do not always correspond to the realities of productions. The "fact" in question concerns the musical's first public Broadway performance—a reasonable locus of our attention, but one that must leave out contingencies such as the show's out-of-town tryouts (it was called *Away We Go!* in its performances in New Haven and did not include what became the show's title song). Nothing in the statement is incorrect— though it matters that hypothetically the statement could indeed be proved false—but it inevitably represents a specific choice among the possible things that may be said.

Another way of putting this is that "facts" matter because they occupy a place in some larger ordering or narrative scheme. As described by the historian Lawrence Stone, narrative requires chronological organization (this does not necessarily exclude temporal shifts such as flashbacks or foreshadowings), the dominant presence of a particular story (though subsidiary stories may be folded into the primary one), description (though more abstract analysis may be interspersed within the description), human agents instead of abstract conditions, and particularities rather than generalities.[3] The requirements of narrative therefore exert pressure on a writer's selection of relevant facts. A vast number of things may be said about *Oklahoma!*, but any given narrative will require only a small percentage of these. In addition, our sense of what matters in a narrative typically depends on notions and commitments that exist prior to our work on that narrative. We never observe anything without some kind of conceptual scheme, implicit or explicit, that allows us to make sense of it—we have, in other words, theories. And it is a mistake to imagine that we can do without either facts or theories; it is a misperception to imagine that the two are fully separate. As musicologist Leo Treitler observes:

> "Facts" come into being only at the moment we assimilate them, for they are orderings of our perceptions, meant to give them coherence. There is therefore no distinct boundary between facts and theories, only lower order and higher order facts. Our traffic with facts is always "theory laden," as Hanson put it. You may feel confident in your possession of a lower order fact—say the date of Mozart's birth—and argue that it is incontestably true quite apart from your knowing it. But that is because the signals are clear, unambiguous, and nonconflicting. [4]

If a fact, to the degree that it is a falsifiable statement that has resisted all challenges, is held to be secure, it still must find a place in the larger network of facts that make up the narrative as a whole. Though explanations require facts, facts by themselves do not constitute explanations. And to consider how explanations work, we must turn to the question of the language that makes up the explanation proper, which requires a brief consideration of the more variable questions of rhetoric, before proceeding to the specific historical inquiry in question.

THE EMPLOTMENT THICKENS

In an influential study of nineteenth-century historical writers, Hayden White argues that historical explanations tended to operate according to three strategies: formal argument, emplotment, and ideological implication.[5] If a chronicle is the ordering of events in time, the "story" can be understood as a shaping or connecting of the events of a chronicle through linguistic gestures of beginning, connecting, or ending. But each story is meaningful because it has a particular kind of plot. White's four principal plot types for historical narratives are Romance, Tragedy, Comedy, and Satire (White, 7–11). The choice of plot—the emplotment—is not the result of the facts on display in the chronicle; rather, the plot helps determine the selection of facts out of the manifold of factual possibilities. Each mode of emplotment tends to reinforce certain points of view; for example, a Romance will most likely emphasize triumphs over adversity, a Comedy will favor reconciliations of the natural and social worlds, a Tragedy will show a terrible (but exemplary) failure, and a Satire will expose the inadequacies of all such views and expectations.

Formal argument, which exists simultaneously with emplotment, seeks to create persuasive explanations by logical deduction and the postulation of general principles that the cases at hand in the narrative are held to fulfill. Again, White takes four styles of argumentation to be the prevailing modes of historical explanation: Formist, Organicist, Mechanistic, and Contextualist. The Formist approach takes on the task of crafting explanations by cataloging the specificities (objects, phenomena, agents, etc.) that create the unique characteristics of a particular historical field; the Organicist approach also works with such specificities but attempts to interrelate them as parts of an overarching whole (this is almost certainly the appropriate locus of the notion of the Zeitgeist, or "spirit of the times); the Mechanistic strategy seeks to understand the specificities of a given historical field as the results of some overarching set of causal laws; the Contextualist strategy sees those same particulars as best explained by the set of contingent relationships that obtain between those very particulars.[6] White's final explanatory quaternity, the mode of ideological implication, offers the political formulations of Anarchism, Conservatism, Radicalism, and Liberalism.[7] These categories do not correspond to specific political groups or platforms but rather indicate a generalized set of attitudes toward such things as social change, or a stance toward the past and future.

The combination of emplotments, modes of argument, and ideological implications produce what White considers historiographical style. He believes that there are natural affiliations between modes. Thus, a Romantic mode of emplotment would combine readily with a Formist mode of argument and an Anarchist mode of ideological implication. By contrast, a Comic mode of emplotment would clash unprofitably with a Mechanistic mode of argument and be confounded utterly if further combined with a Liberal mode of ideological implication. But many historians—many of the most interesting historians—attempt fusions of various modes of explanation in their work.

As for how these modes of explanation can be discerned, White suggests a strong correlation between the kinds of figurative language favored in a narrative and the linked modes of explanation outlined above. Metaphor (relationships of resemblance), metonymy (relationships of contiguity), synecdoche (the equation of parts and wholes, especially in a figurative sense), and irony (the use of words to represent the opposite of their manifest meaning) are all commonly available in any writer's repertory; but Romance will tend to organize itself around metaphorical terms, Comedy will coalesce around the reductions of metonymy, Tragedy will favor the integrative functions of synecdoche, and Satire will show a persistent taste for irony.

Although the analytical categories tallied here may seem excessively schematic, they do serve as useful starting points for a rhetorical analysis of historical writing. But their very literary qualities may cause unease. Where have all the facts gone in this cluster of writerly techniques? What about "objectivity"?

THE WAY WE (ACTUALLY) WERE(N'T)

The nineteenth-century German historian Leopold von Ranke has been endlessly cited for his declaration that the historian's task was to relate the past "as it actually was" (*wie es eigentlich gewesen ist*). Following in Ranke's wake, a strong tradition of historical writing, usually called "positivist history," operated under the claim that facts, as they present themselves to the imagination, can be understood without the conceptual apparatus of rhetoric and philosophical theory. The facts "speak for themselves."[8] A great deal of twentieth-century historiographical writing and reflection, however, has made the notion of "how it actually was" exceedingly problematic. Leaving aside the troublesome intercalation of fact and theory outlined above, even the empirical historical record—the kinds of chronicles that can be assembled—tends to demonstrate an unmanageable degree of diversity in many historical situations. The most likely case is that in almost all historical moments things actually *were* a lot of different ways simultaneously. A historian's selection of facts, because it *must be* only a selection, is already a tacit claim about importance. If we choose to talk about musicals in 1972 by focusing on *Grease* instead of *Pippin*, we are affiliating ourselves with a particular set of narrative possibilities. If we attend to the circumstances of the production rather than the critical reception, we further narrow the scope of our narrative.

There is nothing wrong with these choices; no one can possibly discuss everything. Yet the notion of comprehensiveness, like the notion of absolute impartiality, exerts a beguiling fascination over scholars. And it remains fatally easy for respondents, critics, and reviewers to counter any narrative by protesting, "But what about X? What about Y?" Such criticisms are only productive if the objection carries with it a counterargument, itself open to correction or outright refutation. That is, the historical narratives that we work with as writers and readers—as opposed to chronicles, which can come closer to comprehensiveness (though not impartiality)—actually acquire full value only by being configured within a network of narratives; and this network of narratives is most effective when the various components offer opportunities for conflict as well as support. Historical narratives, like other forms of scholarship, are fundamentally dialogic.

And if the dialogic nature of historical narratives is central to their value, then Hayden White's analysis of historical rhetoric is especially helpful, for it allows us, after registering questions of "factual accuracy," to proceed to the larger claims that a particular narrative may be making about the objects of its study. In the case of the musical, of course, those objects are likely to fall under the rubric of what we usually call "works."

WORKING ON WORKS

The notion that music can take on forms that are more or less stable through time is not recent, of course. Even before the advent of musical notation, which can be taken to fix various aspects of music in at least semi-durable ways, it was possible for musical objects—songs, for instance—to achieve something that might be said to resemble the permanence we would predict of objects like statues or paintings. To the extent that the majority of Western music was, before about 1600, vocal rather than instrumental, music typically approached the condition of texts. Although they were in practice significantly variable, existing on a continuum from the idealized fixity of Scripture to the unrepeatable exuberance of an improvised epic, songs as composite entities (words plus music) could indeed have a long-term existence that arose from their relatively consistent repeatability. One of the interesting things that can be observed in Western music history is the gradual stabilization of musical scores, first in manuscript, then in print culture, then within print culture in particular an increasing tendency to fix aspects of performance (ornaments, dynamics, tempo, articulation, timbre) that had earlier been left open to the oral traditions in which performers were trained. In fact, the musical, because of its complex location between the increasingly text-oriented practices of "classical music" and the improvisatory bent of "popular music," evinces contradictory pulls toward both poles at various moments in its history. But taken as a whole, the historical accounts of the musical have often tended to weigh in on the side of textual stability—seduced, perhaps, by the glamour and prestige associated with the notion of "the musical work."

By around 1800, Western music traditions were increasingly committed to what philosopher Lydia Goehr has called "the work-concept."[9] To offer a quick description, a musical work is an open concept—that is, music classified as a work can actually change with respect to its definition and practical experience under historical circumstances, intimately related with composing/performing/listening practices, without damaging its status as a work—that encourages us to posit an entity that exists "beyond" a score and its specific performances. This is a very big deal. For the purposes of this discussion, in particular, it presents a historical problem, since the kind of musical work

Goehr has in mind is a sort of transcendental object only partially embedded in history. To some extent, this kind of music resembles the kind of art object that seems to have developed in Early Modern Europe in the visual arts: paintings whose manner of execution was at least as important as their object content and whose functions were less devotion and decoration than a kind of protoaesthetic contemplation. And the historiography of art shaped by writings such as Giorgio Vasari's *Lives of the Most Excellent Italian Painters, Sculptors, and Architects*, with its heroic accounts of Leonardo or Michelangelo, arguably presents the original template for later accounts of Artistic Greatness.

Certainly the passion for imagining Great Works by Great Artists (only capitals will do) was especially vivid in the writings of nineteenth-century critics of music and literature, creating notions of artistic potency allied with organic unity (and unitary authorship) that still shape the way many audience members come to value specific musicals. This is all the more important a set of ideas because the musical, almost always overtly collaborative, both challenges and acquiesces to the prestige of Greatness. To take a nineteenth-century comparison: Richard Wagner was an overtly Great Composer: one important measure of his Greatness was his terrifying determination to be a librettist-composer-producer-designer-conductor-director-critic, not some mere musician. His contemporaries W. S. Gilbert and Arthur Sullivan worked together to create operettas, amusing entertainments with an ambivalent attitude toward Greatness: their operettas were certainly works, but they eschewed the lofty, *religioso* tone that surrounded Wagner's operas. Both Wagner and Gilbert & Sullivan ended up with special societies devoted to their works, and strong, even domineering performing traditions. Wagner's high seriousness, his unitary Greatness, has over the years earned him vastly much more ink than Gilbert & Sullivan. And yet, *The Pirates of Penzance* seems to be at least as sturdy as *Parsifal* with respect to its place in the performed repertoire.

Also at stake in the creation of the work is the entangled notion of authorship. For the history of music, this required arguments that placed the composer (not the songwriter, note—and certainly not the performer) as the primary if not the sole progenitor of the work. This was a particularly fraught question for overtly collaborative genres such as opera, all the more because the metaphysical prestige of instrumental music became a core feature of nineteenth-century high culture; it became necessary to preserve the seriousness of opera by reducing the roles of figures such as the librettist, the choreographer, and the major singers. The model for this kind of argument is most eloquently expressed in the major thesis of Joseph Kerman's 1956 book *Opera as Drama*: "the dramatist is the composer."[10]

But to return to the work: an important practical result of the dominance of the work concept, and to the common understanding that works as such can engage with audiences far outside the contexts of their genesis and first performance, is that historians of the musical, like their counterparts in other areas of music or theater studies, continually sit on the horns of a dilemma. Shall we write a *history* of the musical, or a history of the *musical*? In what subtle combination of those terms? What role do our current reactions and responses have in the historical writing we propose to do? Literary critic Northrop Frye once offered a contrast between "ordinary history specializing in the names and dates of authors" versus one "largely concerned with conventions and genres,"[11] and in so doing he pointed at something of the same difficulty. And since our experience of a "work" is so frequently the impetus behind our quest for historical understanding, such that to exclude this response from the writing would be to misrepresent the real stakes of the historical work, how do we balance critical and historical imperatives?

PERIOD PIECE

Related to the problem of potential conflicts between critical and historical approaches is the vexed and vexing difficulty of making persuasive connections between the internal qualities of "works" and the cultural contexts within which they are generated and transmitted. In historical writing about the arts, the difficulty has often been solved by postulating "periods," segments of time and space that are to be regarded as in some way "of a piece." Theater historians may refer to "Restoration theater." Musicologists may talk about "Baroque opera." Art historians may discuss "Impressionism." Periods are in essence a collocation of nonce categories that by common scholarly consensus are treated as more or less stable over time. They may be defined by significant dates, characteristic genres, exemplary artistic figures or groups of figures, terms derived from historical sources, typical contexts of reception, conditions of production, and most important, "style" or "sensibility." More abstractly, they often operate by covertly persuading us that the cultural artifacts of a given period share some kind of underlying "unity."[12] Using Hegel's influential term, they embody a Zeitgeist. Music scholars have long operated with a broad system of classifications such as Medieval, Renaissance, Baroque, Classical, Romantic, and Modern.[13] It is something of a permanent scandal that these terms match very poorly indeed with the same categories as they are manifested in the other arts. But they remain central to historical writing because they have essential practical (i.e., pedagogical) and disciplinary functions.

An activity closely bound up with periodization is the creation of a canon, a repertory of exemplary works that are treated as embodying the essential features of the historical sequence, and are regarded as especially worthy of study and emulation. Again, like periods, canons serve numerous practical and disciplinary functions, and some form of canon is probably unavoidable for scholarly exchange to take place. But it would be a mistake to regard canons as simply traditional, or handed down; canons are normally subject to intense contestation and revision, and the history of canon-making is an integral part of the history of the arts as surely as the history of artists, works, and audiences.

For the history of the musical, perhaps the most characteristic period label is the "Golden Age of the Broadway Musical." The terms that frame the period are already significant because they carry an inherent narrative. There was probably a lesser period before the Golden Age, and there is necessarily a lesser period after it. The archetypal narrative underwriting the Golden Age is the ancient organicist image of birth, flowering/maturity, and decline and fall: a cyclic plot that depends on notions of the seasons as much as it does on a description of the human life cycle. This three-stage archetype is challenged only by the archetype of the continuous progress to the present, often known as "the Whig interpretation of history," after the title of an influential book by English historian Herbert Butterfield.[14] (Bringing White's models of narrative into play, it is easy to see how the organicist archetype could be domesticated for use in Tragedy or Satire, and the Whig archetype could find congruence with Romance or Comedy.)

Moreover, the term "Golden Age," because it is so durably associated with stylistic features such as "the integrated musical," and because it carries a latent association with the intricate sociopolitical frameworks of the United States at the peak of its political and economic flourishing, can be taken to mount a complex argument by analogy about American society at the same time that it purports to restrict itself to matters of art and commerce. In effect, the history of the musical becomes at one level an allegory about the growth, prosperity, and possibly decline of American society. (Whether this be read as Tragedy or Satire presumably depends on your point of view at present.)

Could such notions be done away with entirely? There is no guarantee that rejecting the category of the Golden Age would make a huge difference in the ways that we are accustomed to valuing specific musicals, nor proof that its jettisoning would substantially alter the canon of exemplary works and artists that is gradually coalescing in the scholarly literature on the musical. A more interesting approach than simple rejection would be a close examination of the term and the uses made of it. For the real problem with critical terms comes from their reification; as they harden into unquestioned and unquestionable entities, they come to resemble unquestioned facts in and of themselves instead of tools by which we experiment with points of view.

IN OTHER WORDS

History is at its best an ongoing process of disputation. Like Honoré and Madame Alvarez in *Gigi*, we regale one another with different versions of the story and strive to persuade that our version is the better one, if only for the moment. Unlike Honoré and Mamita, however, our rules of scholarship compel us to pay attention to the corrections and refutations we offer one another. In that way, we aim at improving the effectiveness—the truth, if you will—of our accounts. If this matters to our scholarly scruples, it ought also to matter because of the difference it makes to the objects of our affection. As art critic Dave Hickey has pointed out, every time we speak or write about a particular "work," whether pro or contra, we increase its "value."[15] The value of an artwork is never intrinsic because works are occasions for relationships between people. Each musical bears the imprint of those who speak or write about it because in doing so they magnify it. And such sedimented affections, such accretions of value, are part of doing history, too.[16]

NOTES

1. www.oed.com. Accessed on October 30, 2010.
2. The earliest Chinese narrative history *Zuo Zhuan*, incidentally, is roughly contemporary with histories of Herodotus and Thucycides.
3. Lawrence Stone, "The Revival of Narrative: Reflections on a New Old History" (*Past & Present* [November 1979]: 3–24).
4. Leo Treitler, "The Present as History" (*Perspectives of New Music* 7.2 [Spring–Summer 1969]: 1–58), p. 25.
5. Hayden White, *Metahistory: The Historical Imagination in Nineteenth-Century Europe* (Baltimore: Johns Hopkins University Press, 1973), p. x. The following discussion depends on pp. 1–42.
6. White notes that Formist and Contextualist argumentation is overwhelmingly favored in professional historical writing (White 19–21). I would suggest that histories of the arts tend to be more inclined toward Organicist and Mechanistic modes than "regular" histories.
7. As is the case with the previous formulations, these four are not the only possible positions that may be occupied (White immediately lists Apocalypticism, Reactionism, and Fascism), but they are the dominant modes in the historical writing he considers.
8. Positivist history has been an exceedingly powerful current in both music and theater history. It's worth stressing that this position embodies a number of serious moral claims, such as the value of neutrality as a kind of temporal relativism, and the writer's offer of potential freedom to the reader to make personal sense of the historical account.
9. Lydia Goehr, *The Imaginary Museum of Musical Works: An Essay in the Philosophy of Music* (Oxford: Oxford University Press, 1992).

10. Joseph Kerman, *Opera as Drama, New and Revised Edition* (Berkeley: University of California Press, 1988), p. xv.

11. Northrop Frye, "Literary History" (*New Literary History* 12.2 [Winter 1981]: 219–25).

12. As historian William Weber has pointed out, scholars characterized as "postmodern," though they might be considered opposed to Hegel's totalizing notions, are not necessarily free of the same postulates. See Weber, "Beyond Zeitgeist: Recent Work in Music History" (*Journal of Modern History* 66/2 [June 1994]: 321–25). For that matter, it is certain that to call something "postmodern," inasmuch as it requires a thing called "modern" to define itself, is to remain mired in a totalizing master narrative.

13. Theater history as a discipline has been much more unruly about its categories, which is surely an asset from the point of view of historians of the musical. Lack of consistency gives us greater room to maneuver.

14. Herbert Butterfield, *The Whig Interpretation of History* (London: G. Bell & Sons, 1931).

15. See, for instance, the discussion in Dave Hickey, "Buying the World" (*Daedalus* 131.4 [Fall, 2002]: 69–87).

16. Unsurprisingly, historiography has its own history. A useful introduction is Georg G. Iggers, *Historiography in the Twentieth Century: From Scientific Objectivity to the Postmodern Challenge. With a New Epilogue* (Middletown, CT: Wesleyan University, Press, 2005).

2

Texts and Authors

JIM LOVENSHEIMER

■ □ ■

A 2008 VANDERBILT UNIVERSITY OPERA Theater production was advertised on posters and flyers around campus as
"Kurt Weill's *Street Scene*," which left some wondering what
had become of Elmer Rice and Langston Hughes, authors of
the book and lyrics, respectively. This is hardly an isolated
event; composers routinely receive sole or primary credit for
creating a musical. How many times have the phrases "Leonard
Bernstein's *West Side Story*" (what would Jerome Robbins have
said about that?) or "a Stephen Sondheim musical" been used
to identify a work that in actuality was the result of a collaborative team, whose members share the responsibility for the
musical's success or failure?

Giving privilege to the composer of a musical, or to any other
single collaborator, is problematic in that, when the boundaries
of collaboration are as messy as they often are in the creation of
a musical, the role of any one contributor defies clear definition.
When lyrics are drawn from a passage originally written by the
author of the book, for instance, or when an entire production
is conceived and staged by a choreographer-director whose
work is never written down or recorded, who is the "author,"
and of what? And what, for that matter, is the "text" of a musical for which no single written version exists? The score, after

all, contains little if any dialogue apart from song cues, and the book contains no music. As Stephen Banfield notes, "A musical exists in no definitive form, and a performance is created from no single source."[1] But this raises additional questions: if a performance draws from more than one text, does it in turn create a new cumulative text—what theater theoretician Kier Elam calls a "performance text"—and, if so, who counts as the author or authors of that text?[2] And just what constitutes that cumulative text? Certainly, a performance text must also include the contributions of performers in general and stars in particular; the latter are often thought of as having "created" their roles. Raymond Knapp has suggested that "a performer can create and inflect a character beyond what might be indicated through written words and/or music,"[3] and, as demonstrated later, many stars have been known to re-create, or improvise, from performance to performance, thus suggesting an ongoing authorship that thwarts any finalization of text whatsoever.

Defining the terms "texts" and "authors" with regard to the musical obviously presents multiple challenges, most of which are exacerbated by the genre's collaborative nature. Indeed, the multidisciplinary aspects of the musical make any single theoretical approach incomplete and ultimately unsatisfactory. Musicology, for instance, understandably tends to privilege the musical score over other elements. This approach, which recalls the advertisements for "Kurt Weill's *Street Scene*," is best demonstrated by Joseph P. Swain's *The Broadway Musical: A Critical and Musical Survey*, which in turn takes as its model Joseph Kerman's influential *Opera as Drama*.[4] Kerman argues that, at least in opera, the composer is the dramatist, an argument that when applied to the musical "leads all too easily to the premise that all musicals aspire to the condition of opera" (Banfield, 6). Theater historians and critics, who often still use the term "legitimate theater" for nonmusical plays and thus imply the illegitimacy of musicals, tend to ignore musical theater altogether, although the structuralist approach that dominates theater studies is also valuable for defining critical aspects of the musical, as we shall see. And whereas Roland Barthes introduces the useful term "informational polyphony" to refer to theater's "density of signs" in his essay "Introduction to the Structural Analysis of Narration," he does not go much further than suggesting that the "fundamental problems of semiology are present in the theatre."[5]

Nonetheless, while each of these disciplines offers at best a partial explanation of the musical's multivalent character, all three, when considered together, point toward a more comprehensive understanding of the terms "texts" and "authors" with regard to the musical. That a collaborative genre should require a collaborative critical approach is hardly surprising. As theater and cultural theorist David Savran notes about the musical,

> No form of Western theatre (with the possible exception of opera) uses as many different media to produce a totality that is always far more than the sum of its parts. As a result, analysis requires an implicit or explicit theorization of multiple (and often conflicting) systems of signification.[6]

Only when the seemingly disparate disciplines of literary theory, theater studies, and musicology are deployed to create a cooperative critical system is any headway made toward reaching a satisfactory definition, or definitions, of "texts" and "authors" for use in studying the musical.

TEXTS

For the purposes of this study, a general definition of "texts" can be borrowed, with accretions, from Bernhard Radloff's discussion of the term in the *Encyclopedia of Contemporary Literary Theory*: "a structure [script, musical score, body of dance, scenic design, etc.] composed of elements of signification [words, notes, choreography, etc.] by which the greater or lesser unity of those elements makes itself manifest."[7] Two other terms that sometimes substitute for "text" in practice are "work" and the aforementioned "performance text," which, although sometimes used interchangeably with "text," can also be usefully distinguished. Kier Elam introduces the term "performance text" as follows:

> Unlike the literary semiotician or the analyst of myth or the plastic arts, the researcher in theatre and drama is faced with two quite dissimilar—although immediately correlated—types of textual material: that produced *in* the theatre and that composed *for* the theatre. These two potential focuses of semiotic attention will be indicated as the theatrical or *performance* text and the written or *dramatic* text respectively. (3, emphasis original)

Elam's use of the term demonstrates the influence of the so-called Prague School of the 1930s and 1940s, a group of literary theorists who were among the first to explore the differing sign systems of written dramatic texts and performance contexts. Indeed, in 1940 the Czech theorist Jindřich Honzl made the succinct observation that "dramatic performance is a set of signs,"[8] opening the door to a subsequent distinction between individual dramatic texts—in the musical, the music, lyrics, spoken dialogue, and so on—and the totality, or "set," of their various signs in performance that, together, constitute the performance text, or "work." (Choreography, which technically is not a written text but which acts as a separate element that contributes to the performance text, is arguably one of the several dramatic texts.) Further, this set of signs/performance text/work, identifiable as an object, derives its meanings from the relationships of the individual texts that contribute to it. These relationships can be considered either sympathetic, as in what is often thought of as the integrated musical play model of Rodgers and Hammerstein, or conflicted, as in Scott McMillin's reading of the musical as the product of differences, or friction, between its elements.[9] Either way, the various dramatic texts of the musical do not necessarily relate to each other in any kind of hierarchical system, as the proponents of the composer-dominant approach might have it, but instead produce a some-what egalitarian intertextuality. As Elam observes,

> Each text bears the other's traces, the performance assimilating those aspects of the written play [or score] which the performers choose to transcodify, and the dramatic text being "spoken" [or sung] at every point by the model performance—or [other] possible performances—that motivate it. (190–91)

This intertextuality can be rather slippery in the study of the musical, however, for the dramatic texts are often ephemeral, transitory, or changeable to a degree that can drastically alter the content and subsequent reception of the work.

The Rodgers and Hammerstein musical play was the dominant model for most musicals from 1943 until approximately 1970, and, as mentioned earlier, it is generally discussed in terms of its integration or unity of elements or texts. In his autobiography, Richard Rodgers defined this concept: "When a show works perfectly, it's because all the individual parts complement each other and fit together. No single element overshadows any other. In a great musical, the orchestrations sound the way the costumes look."[10] And for many years the Rodgers and Hammerstein Organization insisted that all productions of the team's works adhere strictly to the written script and score to ensure authorial intent and textual "completeness."

But this model becomes problematic when dealing with any musical, before or after the dominance of Rodgers and Hammerstein, that behaves differently from the model. Theater theoretician Bernard Beckerman notes, "So strong is the contemporary conception of unity that we hesitate to see quite disparate elements as constituting a single work. In thinking of a theatrical production, especially of a play, we assume a coherence of style and manner." But he subsequently (and for our purposes importantly) observes,

> When we regard the entire range of performances, whether of the popular circus or the more austere theatre, we encounter a rich mix of acts. . . . The distinctive American art of the musical theatre includes romantic narrative, songs, dances, and spectacular display. [11]

Beckerman's "rich mix" suggests what musical theater scholar Bruce Kirle, in *Unfinished Show Business*, saw as the key to reading the musical as an "open text," that is, a work that has no definitive form and "precludes the ultimate authority of the text."[12]

Kirle's preceding comment might be made even more precise by substituting "texts" for "text," since authority is found in neither a single element of the musical, as already suggested, nor in the collection of elements that constitutes the performance text. Again, Elam is useful. Recalling Barthes's "density of signs," Elam refers to the theater in general as "the systems of signs, or codes, which produce the performance" (27), adding,

> It is not, clearly, a single-levelled and homogeneous series of signs or signals that emerges, but rather a weave of radically

differentiated modes of expression, each governed by its own selection and combination rules. (39)

Elam's observations recall theater theoretician Manfred Pfister's related observation:

> As a "performed" text, drama [and musicals], in contrast to purely literary texts, makes use not only of verbal, but also acoustic and visual codes. It is a "synaesthetic text." This important criterion provides the starting point for any semiotic analysis of drama. [13]

When the emphasis on various modes of expression in a musical is different in productions subsequent to the original, the performance text changes, sometimes profoundly, and this potential for alteration and new meanings leads Kirle to categorize the performance text, as well as the varied dramatic texts, as "open," or without ultimate authority. "Musicals wed text, performance, and reception," Kirle observes in his opening sentence, "to create meaning within specified historical contexts" (1). In other words, an "authoritative" performance text is impossible, for even if a musical were recreated as an exact replica of its original production, its performance text would be altered, or open, by virtue of a different historical context. And sometimes a revisionist production, coupled with a different social, cultural, or economic climate, can create a new work altogether. Terry Eagleton, writing of philosopher Hans-Georg Gadamer, explains,

> As the work passes from one cultural or historical context to another, new meanings may be culled from it which were perhaps never anticipated by its author or contemporary audience.... All interpretation is situational, shaped and constrained by the historically relative criteria of a particular culture. [14]

For instance, the extremely successful revival of *Chicago* eliminates Bob Fosse's original spectacular production aesthetic and instead presents the show in a minimalist scenic environment. But it also takes on additional layers of meaning for audiences who have experienced the show business–driven trials of O. J. Simpson and the late Michael Jackson, events that long postdate the original production.

Kirle's argument for the musical as an open text recalls similar arguments in musicologist Richard Taruskin's *Text and Act*, in which he criticizes musicologists promoting the Early Music movement as misguidedly clinging to the idea

> of the reified *Werk*—the objectified musical work-thing to which fidelity is owed. . . . Although easily distinguished from performance, which is ephemeral and contingent, the notion of "the (timeless) work," as it has been called . . . is not easily disengaged from that of the (permanent) text through which it is transmitted. [15]

He continues a few pages later with an observation that becomes an integral element of Kirle's defense of the pre-Rodgers and Hammerstein musical: "The whole trouble with Early Music as a 'movement' is the way it has uncritically accepted the post-Romantic work-concept and imposed it anachronistically on pre-Romantic repertories" (13). Kirle has a similar complaint:

> Formalistic histories have tended to regard nonintegrated, pre-Rodgers and Hammerstein musicals as unfinished or open texts and assumed their artistic inferiority while privileging the artistic aspirations of the post-Rodgers and Hammerstein texts as closed, autonomous, and artistically superior. (1)

Needless to say, Kirle does not uphold that implied superiority.

AUTHORS

Kirle raises another important issue related to the texts of musicals that provides a transition to the equally thorny subject of authorship. After observing that the British producer Cameron Mackintosh "brags that his productions [of the same show] are interchangeable," Kirle complains that "interchangeable, duplicate productions seem more like mass-produced technology than theatre" (10). He goes on to contrast what he calls Mackintosh's "übermarionette school of musical theatre" with the individualized and often improvisatory nature of actors' performances in musical comedy. In the latter, Kirle suggests, the actors are "cocreators," which in turn implies the co-authorship alluded to earlier. In 1927, for example, Charles Winninger, as Captain Andy in *Show Boat*, acted out the remainder of a melodrama when roughnecks in the onstage audience interrupted the performance. "No one today is quite sure exactly what Winninger did or how long the specialty lasted," Kirle observes, because, while Winninger's specialty was part of the performance text, it was never part of the written dramatic text (38). Instead, the actor created it, differently, perhaps, from performance to performance. In a more recent example, Harvey Fierstein, during his tenure as a frumpy Baltimore housewife in *Hairspray*, improvised nightly with his co-star Dick Latessa, adding lines and bits of business that amused the audience as well as Latessa. Both of these "additions" might be seen as violations of the written texts, but most audiences enthusiastically accepted them as part of the performance text, as did the creators of the written texts. The contributions of the actors in these examples, separated as they are by seventy-five years, indicate how a completely ephemeral aspect of performance can confer co-authorship on the actor. That transference of authorship is not always approved by other authors, however: Kirle points out that soon after *Fiddler on the Roof* opened on Broadway, star Zero Mostel "started interpolating stage business and ad-libs," much to the chagrin of director Jerome Robbins and librettist Joseph Stein (34).

Even without improvisation, performance is a creative act. Further, because various external elements—different audiences, locations, contemporaneous events, and so on—often alter aspects of performance, no two performances are ever quite the same, even if they are intended to replicate previous performances. This in turn implies two related ideas: (1) because performance is fundamentally creative, it is at all times an integral part of the performance text, and (2) the performer is a coauthor of that text.

These examples of co-creation demonstrate what Pfister refers to as "the sociology of authorship" (29). Pfister, who is writing about non–musical theater but whose observations apply with equal accuracy to the musical, notes:

> As far as dramatic texts are concerned, the sociology of authorship becomes even more complicated in view of the multiplicity of productive functions. That is, the author of the printed and literary text substratum is no more than one of the several "authors" of the multimedial, enacted text. (29)

The importance of this differentiation of authorship cannot be overestimated. How accurate is it, for instance, to refer to "Rodgers and Hammerstein's *Oklahoma!*" when one of the most memorable and discussed aspects of the original production was choreographer Agnes de Mille's uniquely balletic dances? Her work was, and continues to be, appreciated, but although she created an identifiable physical style for the work, she is rarely given *authorial* credit, perhaps in part because her dances were never part of a written text. Further, when Trevor Nunn directed his influential 1998 revival of the work at London's National Theatre, he replaced all of de Mille's dances as well as the original dance music while keeping the rest of the script and score, although not the orchestrations, virtually intact. De Mille's co-authorship of the work (and that of orchestrator Robert Russell Bennett) literally disappeared.

This disappearance of an author recalls Roland Barthes's important 1967 essay, "The Death of the Author." Seeking to reexamine and resituate the reader's role in the text, Barthes argues that "a text is made of multiple writings," further noting that "the reader is the space on which all the quotations that make up a writing are inscribed without any of them being lost; a text's unity lies not in its origins but in its destination."[16] This perspective links Barthes with other reception theorists, who shift the primary importance of a text from the author to the reader. Writing about an even earlier work—Jean-Paul Sartre's *What Is Literature?* (1948)— Terry Eagleton observes that "a work's reception is never just an 'external' fact about it, a contingent matter of book reviews and book shop sales [or, I would add, for the musical, out-of-town preview responses, newspaper reviews, and box-office sales]. It is a constitutive dimension of the work itself."[17] Thirty years later in *The Act of Reading*, Wolfgang Iser writes of the "strategies" and "codes" in texts that must be understood before the reader can construct meanings from those texts.[18] Similarly, the conventions of the musical must be understood and accepted by audiences ("readers") before any meaning can be created. When these conventions are replaced by a new set of codes, audiences, like readers of literary works, often have difficulty constructing meaning. (Here I am reminded of a confused woman overheard during the intermission of *Spring Awakening*, a 2006 musical that radically rethought the use of song, dance, and narrative in adapting Frank Wedekind's late nineteenth-century tale of adolescent sexuality: "I just don't understand it: it's not at all like *The Boy from Oz*.")

Following Barthes's essay by a year, Michel Foucault's "What Is an Author?" reconfigures the author-reader-text relation from a slightly more complex perspective. "A certain number of notions that are intended to replace the privileged position of the author," Foucault notes, "actually seem to preserve that privilege and suppress the real meaning of his disappearance."[19] He then proceeds to reassess the author within, and without, his or her texts, observing the following:

> [An] author's name is not simply an element in a discourse. . . .
> [I]t performs a certain role with regard to narrative discourse,
> assuring a classificatory function. Such a name permits one to
> group together a certain number of texts, define them, differ-
> entiate them from and contrast them to others. In addition, it
> establishes a relationship among the texts. . . . The author's name
> serves to characterize a certain mode of being of discourse. (147)

Foucault's observation that an authorial identity allows the grouping of texts—for our purposes, and despite their inaccuracies or incompleteness, "Rodgers and Hammerstein shows," "Sondheim musicals," or "Bob Fosse musicals," and so on—is important. He calls such authorial identities "founders of discursivity," and he observes that they are "unique in that they are not just the authors of their own works. They have produced something else: the possibilities and the rules for the formation of other texts" (154). For instance, how many shows after 1943 can be identified, in Foucault's sense, as "Rodgers and Hammerstein musicals" although that writing team had nothing to do with their creation? Creating a musical in the 1940s and 1950s that was not influenced by Rodgers and Hammerstein was virtually impossible: if a show did not follow the model, it recalled the model as something against which to react. And few reactions against the model lasted long on Broadway stages until the late 1960s (*Cabaret*, 1966;

Hair, 1968) or the early 1970s (*Company*, 1970). In another application of Foucault's classification, however, we may note the number of musicals that, despite their being created by the same person, do *not* produce possibilities for other texts. Despite having written the scores to a number of Broadway hits, for instance, Elton John has yet to be recognized as the founder of a discourse within the musical. There is no such term as "an Elton John musical."

By the end of his essay, however, Foucault is prepared to acknowledge the disappearance, if not the death, of the author. In his penultimate paragraph, he observes the following:

> Although, since the eighteenth century, the author has played the role of the regulator of the fictive ... still, given the historical modifications that are taking place, it does not seem necessary that the author-function remain constant in form, complexity, and even in existence. I think that, as our society changes, at the very moment when it is in the process of changing, the author-function will disappear, and in such a manner that fiction and its polysemic texts will once again function according to another mode, but still with a system of constraint—one which will no longer be the author, but which will have to be determined or, perhaps, experienced. (159–60)

Any new system of constraint, or understanding, that develops as a tool for critically responding to the musical will be based at least in part on the assumption that each audience member brings his or her own social and historical identity to the experience of any given show. Because of the open nature of a musical's text, both in terms of how it can be changed by its creators and/or interpreters and how it must of necessity be perceived differently according to the historical period in which it is experienced, its reception will always be a part of its meaning. This in turn implies that the audience, individually and collectively, will always play a role in its creation and re-creation.

SHOW BOAT: A CASE STUDY

The problems of definitively establishing text and author are perhaps best found in a number of much-revived and often rewritten "classic" musicals. To be sure, that designation is in itself problematic and often ironic, in that most such shows have undergone many changes since their first productions, so that the qualities that earn them "classic" status may have been long since excised in revivals. Nonetheless, older repertory shows provide particularly useful case studies for the problems considered above. Although any number of pre–Rodgers and Hammerstein musicals might serve in this regard, *Show Boat* is the outstanding example of a "classic" that has never been performed the same way in any two productions, a circumstance that brings the issue of its "text" to the forefront. Moreover, given that all productions—even the original—use songs not by Jerome Kern or Oscar Hammerstein II, the official composer and lyricist of the score, problems of authorship arise even beyond the issues raised earlier.

When *Show Boat* opened in 1927, it was generally agreed by critics and audiences to be a giant step forward for the American musical in terms of the genre at last becoming "serious." Although Hammerstein wrote a book that contained elements of musical comedy as well as of the operettas for which he was mostly known, he also allowed for spaces of actor co-authorship, such as Charles Winninger's comic business discussed earlier or Norma Terris's impersonations of contemporaneous entertainers. (Terris was Magnolia, the principal female character.) And, as Scott McMillin found in a previously overlooked early draft for *Show Boat*, Hammerstein and Kern, in fashioning the role of Joe specifically for Paul Robeson, created a second act scene that was to be a performance of interpolated spirituals.[20] Indeed, as Todd Decker has noted, the scene was called "A Paul Robeson Recital," thus acknowledging the centrality of the performer to the early concept of the work.[21] Nonetheless, the "text" of *Show Boat*, in 1927, was probably considered a fait accompli once the show opened. But the history of the show's revivals suggests that it was an open text almost from the beginning and demonstrates the difficulty of establishing any kind of textual authority for this or any other show.

Show Boat was first revived by Florenz Ziegfeld in 1932. Hoping to bolster his failing finances, Ziegfeld recruited many of the original cast members and replaced several with even bigger names. Paul Robeson, for instance, who turned down the original production but created a sensation as Joe in the later London production, was cast in the revival, although no attempt was made to reinstate the recital of spirituals. The production was as close to a replication of the original as possible. When it toured, however, it was increasingly truncated, first by cuts in the cast and finally in massive cuts to the show itself, which resulted in a ninety-minute version that played between features in movie palaces. According to Miles Kreuger, Hammerstein's assistant did the cutting.[22] While the 1936 film version closely followed the original stage version, the postwar 1946 revival brought changes indicative of a new era for the American musical.

The elements of operetta and musical comedy that had fused with great success in the original production at this point seemed dated in the wake of Hammerstein's own advancement of the form in *Oklahoma!* (1943) and *Carousel* (1945). When composer Jerome Kern died before the revival began rehearsals, Hammerstein took over the entire production. In a note for the cast album of the revival, Hammerstein made a telling comment: "Our present production had to be built to match the enhanced glamour of the public's memory of Ziegfeld's original production" (Kreuger, 158). Hammerstein was reimagining the work to fit the *memory* of the audience's reception, and this resulted in major changes to the show's look. Kreuger notes,

> Because of Hammerstein's concern that the public in 1946 had come to expect a more decorative look [in musicals], there was a conscious effort to brighten the sets and costumes. In both color and form, the mounting was intentionally theatrical and artificial, thereby setting a trend for designing *Show Boat* on stage and screen that has lasted until today. (158)

Robert Russell Bennett updated the orchestrations, and while Hammerstein wrote in playbills that the script and score were largely "as they were when originally written in 1927," the cuts and changes were actually far more substantial than this comment suggests. The script was also trimmed of language that, in terms of race, was less acceptable in 1946 than it had been in 1927. The word "nigger," for instance, which occurred throughout the original script, was virtually eliminated. Finally, as a response to the impact of Agnes de Mille's influential use of dance in the first three Rodgers and Hammerstein musicals, much dance was added to the revival. Indeed, Kreuger refers to its "preoccupation with dance" (163). The changes that Hammerstein made to his earlier work, in general, were attempts to re-cast it in the mold of the Rodgers and Hammerstein musical play, a form that was codified only three years earlier. Even Hammerstein could not avoid being influenced by his own accomplishments.

Show Boat has experienced major overhauls with each new revival. The most recent Broadway production, directed by

Harold Prince in 1994, contained a new second act sequence created by Prince and choreographer Susan Stroman. Prince also redistributed some of the musical numbers, most notably giving "Why Do I Love You," originally sung by Gaylord and Magnolia, to Parthy, played by Elaine Stritch. And just six years earlier, conductor John McGlinn, aided by numerous materials uncovered in a Secaucus, New Jersey, warehouse, recorded all the known music ever written for any production of the show. But while the result is a valuable collection of Kern and Hammerstein's efforts and reveals countless alterations made to the work throughout its history, those changes remain disconnected artifacts and argue against any "definitive" or authoritative versions. As Kreuger notes,

> Although the show's earliest alterations were made by Hammerstein himself as a method of keeping the work vital to a changing audience, the trend was begun to permit the show to follow whatever theatrical vogue might have been fashionable. Like an older building that has been "modernized" through the elimination of its distinctive architectural details, *Show Boat* has been left without its original form and with only diluted dramatic impact. (212)

Kreuger ends his consideration of the work with the hope that "perhaps the time has come to re-create *Show Boat* in the form that inspired *New York Telegram* critic Robert Garland to call it on opening night simply 'an American masterpiece'" (213).

The irony of Kreuger's wish is that, as we have observed, such a re-creation is impossible. And even if it were possible, would it be desirable? Apart from institutionalizing the work as a museum artifact, what would be the point of reverting to the 1927 version? Even if the original script and score could be replicated, the work would evoke vastly different responses from a post–civil rights movement, post–Rodgers and Hammerstein audience. These responses in turn would change the performance text, regardless of the dramatic texts that were used.

In 1927, the interpolation of musical numbers that were not created for the show into which they were inserted was still a common practice, and *Show Boat* contains several examples of this practice. Later versions of the show continued the practice and inserted other numbers, but two of the principal songs interpolated into the original production were Charles K. Harris's hit "After the Ball" and "Bill," a song by Kern and lyricist P. G. Wodehouse originally featured in the 1917 musical *Oh Lady! Lady!* (Sousa's "Washington Post" is also used to introduce the rehearsal scene in act 2 that contains "Bill.") The placement of the songs makes their use somewhat appropriate. In the second act, for instance, Julie rehearses "Bill" in the nightclub where she works, and, later in the act, Magnolia sings "After the Ball" at a New Year's Eve celebration, a deliberately nostalgic choice even in the onstage setting. But the presence of the songs, however appropriate their settings, presents a problem in terms of establishing authorship. Only Kern and Hammerstein get billing for having written the score, and while Wodehouse and Harris get credit for their contributions in the published score and in most programs, the musical text is nonetheless more collaborative than is generally known by most of the theatergoing public. The songs add period "authority" to the show even as they implicitly question the authority of the acknowledged composer and lyricist.

David Savran raises issues and questions appropriate to consider here:

> In the field of cultural production, problems of text and performance open up a number of crucially important questions for a history of popular-theatre forms: How can claims of authenticity obtain when original texts have disappeared as well as the

performance styles and traditions that made the pieces work? If musicals are the most collaborative and conventionalized of theatrical forms, what is the value of a theory of authorship? Does it suffice to describe *Lady in the Dark* (1941) as a Kurt Weill musical? Or as a Kurt Weill-Ira Gershwin-Moss Hart-Gertrude Lawrence musical? Or does one need to mobilize a different model of cultural production? Perhaps one in which questions of authorship are displaced from the individual maker to a collective subject? Or to the history of conventions? Or to the class habitus of the producers? (214)

As we have seen, the disciplines of literary theory, theater theory and history, and musicology all inform the consideration of these and other questions that are unique to the musical. All of them share Savran's impulse toward considering the author of a musical as, to use his term, "a collective subject," although musicology is the slowest to embrace this idea. And all three of them have begun to deal with the issue of closed versus open texts, especially in terms of works for the stage. But the questions are still being discussed, and no definitive answers are as yet forthcoming.

In the end, while we may know who wrote the book, music, and lyrics for any given musical, the knowledge of who the author is (or authors are) might be slightly harder to discern, especially if, as members of the audience, we are part of the collective authorship. And figuring out what the text is has a great deal to do with when and how we experience any given performance. The difficulty of these issues is real, but they must be dealt with by anyone who cares about the musical. As the musical undergoes more and more serious critical interrogation, solutions to the problems posed in this essay might be forthcoming. But even if they are not, the problems make for challenging consideration.

NOTES

1. Stephen Banfield, *Sondheim's Broadway Musicals* (Ann Arbor: University of Michigan Press, 1993), p. 3.
2. Kier Elam, *The Semiotics of Theatre and Drama*, 2nd ed. (London: Routledge, 2002), p. 3.
3. Raymond Knapp, *The American Musical and the Formation of National Identity* (Princeton, NJ: Princeton University Press, 2005), p. 190.
4. Joseph P. Swain, *The Broadway Musical; A Critical and Musical Survey*, 2nd ed. (Lanham, MD: Scarecrow Press, 2002), and Joseph Kerman, *Opera as Drama*, rev. ed. (London: Faber and Faber, 1988).
5. Roland Barthes, "Introduction to the Structural Analysis of Narration," in *Image, Music, Text*, ed. and trans. Stephen Heath (New York: Hill and Wang, 1977, 261–67), p. 262.
6. David Savran, "Toward a Historiography of the Popular" (*Theatre Survey* 45.2 [November 2004]: 211–17), pp. 215–16.
7. Bernhard Radloff, "Text," in *Encyclopedia of Contemporary Literary Theory: Approaches, Scholars, Terms*, ed. Irena R. Makaryk (Toronto: University of Toronto Press, 1993, 639–41), p. 639.
8. Jindřich Honzl, "Dynamics in the Sign in the Theater," in *Semiotics of Art: Prague School Contributions*, ed. L. Matejka and K. Pomorsak (Cambridge, MA: MIT Press, 1976, 74–93), p. 74.
9. Scott McMillin, *The Musical as Drama: A Study of the Principles and Conventions behind Musical Shows from Kern to Sondheim* (Princeton, NJ: Princeton University Press, 2006).
10. Richard Rodgers, *Musical Stages: An Autobiography* (New York: Random House, 1975), p. 227.
11. Bernard Beckerman, *Theatrical Presentation: Performer, Audience, and Act* (London: Routledge, 1990), p. 90.
12. Bruce Kirle, *Unfinished Show Business: Broadway Musicals as Works-in-Process* (Carbondale: Southern Illinois University Press, 2005), p. 7.
13. Manfred Pfister, *The Theory and Analysis of Drama*, trans. John Halliday (Cambridge: Cambridge University Press, 1988), p. 7.

14. Terry Eagleton, *Literary Theory: An Introduction,* 2nd ed. (Minneapolis: University of Minnesota Press, 1996), pp. 61–62.

15. Richard Taruskin, *Text and Act: Essays on Music and Performance* (New York: Oxford University Press, 1995), pp. 10–11.

16. Roland Barthes, "The Death of the Author," in *Image, Music, Text,* ed. and trans. Stephen Heath (New York: Hill and Wang, 1977, 142–48), p. 148.

17. See Eagleton, 72, and Jean-Paul Sartre, *What Is Literature?* trans. Bernard Frechtman (London: Routledge, 2001).

18. Wolfgang Iser, *The Act of Reading: A Theory of Aesthetic Response* (Baltimore: Johns Hopkins University Press, 1980).

19. Michel Foucault, "What Is an Author?" in *Textual Strategies: Perspectives in Post-Structuralist Criticism,* ed. and trans. Josué V. Harari (Ithaca, NY: Cornell University Press, 1979, 141–60), p. 143.

20. Scott McMillin, "Paul Robeson, Will Vodery's 'Jubilee Singers,' and the Earliest Script of the Kern-Hammerstein *Show Boat*" (*Theatre Survey* 41 [2000]: 51–70), p. 66.

21. See Todd Decker, "'Do You Want to Hear a Mammy Song?' A Historiography of *Show Boat*" (*Contemporary Theatre Review* 19.1 [2009]: 8–21), pp. 20–21. Decker provides a more in-depth discussion of this interpolation in "Black/White Encounters on the American Stage and Screen (1924–2005)" (Ph.D. dissertation, University of Michigan, 2007), pp. 116–23.

22. Miles Kreuger, *Show Boat: The Story of a Classic American Musical* (New York: Da Capo Press, 1977), p. 108.

3

Musical Styles
and Song Conventions

PAUL R. LAIRD

■ ◻ ■

THE MUSICAL THEATER DEMANDS THAT composers provide immediately accessible music in a variety of styles. Once a stage character reaches that magical moment when talking stops and singing begins, what she or he sings must be stylistically comprehensible to the audience. In a 1920s show, for example, two characters might be about to declare their love and the orchestra will begin a waltz. Or a secondary character might show the audience a new dance that corresponds to a song's name, opening with a spoken and sung verse before the chorus (or refrain) in a rapid duple meter with frequent syncopation. In a modern show, a dramatic moment might call for a rock style that will be declared by the drummer and electric guitar. Another song in the same show might be more contemplative, and the relaxed string accompaniment and brushes on the cymbals signal a traditional Broadway ballad.

Composers seeking appropriate music for the American musical theater since the late nineteenth century have used many styles. Although popular music has changed greatly over the years, some old musical styles have stayed current in the theater longer than one might expect. The waltz, for example, was passé as a couples dance by 1900 but remained significant as a theatrical song type throughout the twentieth century. This essay considers representative musical styles and types of songs that have appeared theatrically since the late nineteenth century. Some are primarily styles, such as jazz, which has been a profound influence on Broadway musicals and films since the 1920s, and ragtime, which denotes a style expressed in its purest form in rags. A number of composers, however, especially Irving Berlin, wrote songs in the 1910s and 1920s that used stylistic elements of ragtime while not being in the form of a rag. Similar distinctions could be made about blues and other musical styles. Also relevant are many dance types, such as the waltz and polka, which may carry dramatic associations, influence a composer's choice of meter, and shape melodic and rhythmic expectations.

In *The American Musical Theater* (1975), Lehman Engel provides a useful typology for songs in musicals.[1] Engel describes the importance of a show's opening musical number and the different approaches taken in this song type by various creators. He notes that the musical soliloquy, when a character lays bare inner feelings, is important to both opera and the musical. The ballad, usually a slower number with a memorable melody and often associated with love or another emotion, has been a staple for popular song composers. Engel coins the term "charm song," defined as "a song that embodies generally delicate, optimistic, and rhythmic music, and lyrics of light though not necessarily comedic subject matter" (87). He names "The Surrey with the Fringe on Top" from *Oklahoma!* as the archetypical charm song. The musical scene is a long segment "in which the words shifted back and forth between dialogue and lyric (sung) verse" (89). Engel traces its origins to grand opera and operetta, and shows the significant place it holds in a number of shows where the creators tell the audience much about characters and move the plot forward. Engel also describes the importance of comedic songs in musicals. A some-what less convincing general category that Engel offers is the "rhythm song," which is "carried along, or propelled by, a musical beat which is most usually a regular one" (106). He also shows the importance of distributing the various song types across a show's musical program (109–22), and devotes an entire chapter to Broadway opera (132–54).

Broadway conventions also include other song types, such as the "I want" song and "eleven-o-clock number." The first takes place early in a show and discloses a main character's primary motivation, such as "Wouldn't It Be Loverly?" from *My Fair Lady* and "The Wizard and I" from *Wicked*. The so-called eleven-o-clock number goes back to a day when curtain times were later, and at about this hour a show included a number that heightened the energy level or dramatic interest in the second act. Examples include "Sit Down, You're Rocking the Boat" from *Guys and Dolls* and "You've Got to Be Carefully Taught" from *South Pacific*. Usually each act also ends with a strong number. Powerful act finales in recent shows include "Defying Gravity" in *Wicked* (Act 1) and "You Can't Stop the Beat" from *Hairspray* (Act 2), but it would be very difficult to generalize about musical style in finales.

The most typical popular song form used on Broadway is a verse followed by a chorus or refrain. A verse is often rendered in speech rhythms, often over a simple, chordal accompaniment, somewhat like operatic recitative. It is not commonly the verse that communicates stylistic information about the music. That comes in the chorus, which might range from a fast dance tempo to a slow ballad. It is also the chorus that a listener remembers; there are many famous songs for musical theater for which only the most rabid of fans know the verse. Typical forms of choruses appear below in the description of ballads.

RICHES FROM RAGS TO RAP: THE DEVELOPMENT OF MUSICAL STYLES

The first popular musical style to emanate from African Americans and become a national craze was ragtime, popular from the early 1890s to about World War I. In a deliberate duple meter with syncopated melodies, rags by Scott Joplin and others influenced commercial songwriters to compose pieces, sometimes called rags, that imitated aspects of the style but did not carry all markers of the type. These songs usually had syncopated melodies, ragtime's most distinctive feature. Irving Berlin wrote a number of such songs, most famously "Alexander's Ragtime Band" (1911). Berlin wrote a Broadway score that included samples of his version of ragtime in *Watch Your Step* (1914). The first act finale was "The Syncopated Walk." Later musicals included ragtime references to help set a time and place. In *Show Boat* (1927), "Goodbye, My Lady Love" sounds like a rag, and there is also a reference to the style in the dance of "Shipoopi" from *The Music Man* (1957), a story that takes place just before World War I, making ragtime a useful stylistic signifier (⬤ Example 3.1).

An operetta score might include a variety of musical types, from the familiar strains of the waltz and march to contemporary popular music. *The Desert Song* (1926), for example, included numbers by Sigmund Romberg based on the genre's typical European roots, but also "It," which might have appeared in a contemporary musical comedy (⬤ Example 3.2). Despite this musical variety, however, the dominant stylistic expectation in an operetta was lyrical melodies composed for trained voices. The source for this style was opera, and many operetta performers had operatic training and might even have had a parallel career on the operatic stage. Emma Trentini, who sang with the Manhattan Opera Company, for example, appeared as the female lead in Victor Herbert's *Naughty Marietta* (1910) and other operettas. Herbert and other operetta composers wrote songs for stars like Trentini that featured a wide range, large leaps, delicate ornamentation, and other virtuoso touches. Famous examples of such writing include the "Italian Street Song" from *Naughty Marietta*, "Serenade" from *The Student Prince*, and "You Are Love" for *Show Boat*, a musical play that included touches from operetta models (🔊 Example 3.3). Even after the operetta declined in popularity in the 1930s, the style remained familiar; for example, Bernstein's *Candide* (1956), was described as an operetta and includes the operatic "Glitter and Be Gay."

Opera itself has also appeared on Broadway. This style includes virtuosic vocal writing for large voices and major segments of the show that are sung throughout. The most famous opera on Broadway was George Gershwin's *Porgy and Bess* (1935), with vocal demands on the major characters necessitating that the show be double or triple cast for Broadway runs with eight performances per week. Other operas that have appeared on Broadway include Marc Blitzstein's *Regina* (1949) and Gian Carlo Menotti's *The Consul* (1950) and *The Saint of Bleecker Street* (1954). It should be noted that the original version of Sondheim's *Sweeney Todd* (1979) and several megamusicals of the 1980s fit part of the genre's definition, being mostly sung and featuring large stage spectacle. Schoenberg and Boublil's *Les Misérables* (1985) and Andrew Lloyd Webber's *Phantom of the Opera* (1986) both include lengthy segments that are entirely sung and offer rich technical effects, and the latter includes true operatic scenes.

Jazz emerged as a popular musical style after World War I, and it was a major influence on musical theater. As a style, jazz has changed throughout its history, but the type that had the most influence on other music is swing of the 1930s. One can trace jazz influence on the musical theater before swing appeared, however. One of the first appearances of jazz gestures in a Broadway show was in *Shuffle Along* (1921), the first Broadway show conceived entirely by African Americans. Eubie Blake's score (lyrics by Noble Sissle) included rich syncopation and other jazz-like elements (probably with little improvisation). The point was made in the first song entitled "I'm Simply Full of Jazz," and other major songs included "Love Will Find a Way," "Bandana Days," "I'm Just Wild about Harry," and "Baltimore Buzz" (◉ Example 3.4). There was even a song in the second act called "Syncopation Stenos." After *Shuffle Along*, the sounds of jazz never left Broadway, but usually served as a novelty to add color to a score. A show that had a strong jazz feel was the African American *Hot Chocolates* (1929), with a score by Fats Waller and others, and with Louis Armstrong in the cast. George Gershwin brought jazz rhythms and blues intervals to the musical theater, but his music lacked the improvisation that most scholars believe a part of true jazz. His use of jazz rhythms appears in "Fascinating Rhythm" from *Lady, Be Good* (1924). A number of the composer's scores continued in this vein, including *Porgy and Bess*. During the swing era and later, typical Broadway orchestration resembled that of the big band (but also with strings), and orchestrators routinely used big band sounds. Later jazz styles, such as bop and free jazz, appeared less often on Broadway, but Leonard Bernstein made telling use of modern jazz sounds in *West Side Story*, especially in the song "Cool," reminiscent of music by the Modern Jazz Quartet (◉ Example 3.5). Jazz of earlier periods has appeared in several shows based on prominent musicians, including, for example, Fats Waller's songs in *Ain't Misbehavin'* (1978), Duke Ellington's tunes in *Sophisticated Ladies* (1981), and the music of Jelly Roll Morton in *Jelly's Last Jam* (1992).

Like jazz, the influence of blues in other areas of American concert music and musical theater has been more in use of the style's typical sounds than in its pure, improvisational form.

Early blues figures, such as Ma Rainey and Bessie Smith, seldom if ever appeared on Broadway, although Smith was in the short-lived *Pansy* (1929). Far more important for the musical theater, and films as well, has been the appearance of the genre's distinctive melodic and harmonic gestures appearing in songs and instrumental numbers that are not in a typical blues form, like the famed 12-bar progression. Gershwin, for example, made routine use of blues melodic gestures in his melodies, such as the lowered third, fifth, and seventh degrees of the scale. One of his typical bluesy melodies is "Sam and Delilah" from *Girl Crazy* (1930), and a very famous example of a blues third in his output occurs in the closing gesture in *An American in Paris* (1928), which appeared as a ballet score in the 1951 MGM film by the same name (● Example 3.6). Jerome Kern exemplified typical theatrical use of the blues in "Can't Help Lovin' Dat Man" from *Show Boat*. The song works well in the langorous tempo often associated with the genre and includes blues notes in the melody, but the typical harmonic gestures for the style occur only in the verse.[2] Blues had a huge influence on later popular styles that have appeared in musical theater, such as rhythm and blues and rock.

Folk music has been an occasional influence on musical theater and films, often appearing in shows where the plot or a particular character renders such music appropriate. Examples include the song "Edelweiss" from *The Sound of Music* (1959), a simple song that comes to represent Austria in that story, and "Next to Lovin' (I Like Fightin')" from *Shenandoah* (1975), among other tunes in that show, which involves a Virginia family during the American Civil War (● Example 3.7). These songs both feature the diatonic, singable melodies one associates with most folk music. "Ol' Man River" from *Show Boat* (1927), with its moving melody and powerful lyrics that capture the Mississippi River's significance in the story, carries a potent folk essence (mingled with the nineteenth-century spiritual), but the demands on the baritone are unlike those of most folk songs. Country music, with a musical character that often resembles folk music, also appears in musical theater, with two good examples being "Shoeless Joe from Hannibal, Mo." (with the character of a hoedown) from *Damn Yankees* (1955) and much of the score of *Big River* (1985), by noted country musician Roger Miller (🔊 Example 3.8). English shows have included songs with folk characteristics as well, such as "Who Will Buy?" from *Oliver!* (1960) and "Deep into the Ground" from *Billy Elliot* (2005). *The Secret Garden* (1991), with music by Lucy Simon, takes place in the English countryside with several local characters, and its score is filled with references to English folk songs, especially the lowered seventh scale degree found in the modes that dominate folk music.

"Ol' Man River" from *Show Boat*, as noted above, sounds somewhat like a nineteenth-century African American spiritual, and Broadway composers also have occasionally alluded to the revival number, another type of inspirational song often found in religious music. Revival songs musically bear some resemblance to gospel music, and they have usually appeared in musicals for humorous, ironic effect, such as "Blow, Gabriel, Blow" from Cole Porter's *Anything Goes* (1934), Frank Loesser's "Sit Down, You're Rockin' the Boat" from *Guys and Dolls* (1950), and "Brotherhood of Man" from *How to Succeed in Business without Really Trying* (1961; 🔊 Example 3.9). Stephen Schwartz also included similar numbers in his score to *Godspell* (1971), such as "We Beseech Thee."

Various types of Latin music, especially dances, have made frequent appearances in the musical theater. While careful distinctions can be made between Latin music from different countries and traditions, the simple truth about its theatrical use—as in other Western music—is that many composers treat all influences from the Spanish- and Portuguese-speaking worlds as if from one source. Examples of this tendency include

Frederick Loewe's composition of an Argentine tango for "The Rain in Spain" in *My Fair Lady* (1956) when textual references in the song clearly point to Iberia, and in *West Side Story* (1957), in which the Latin characters are Puerto Rican, but the composer Bernstein used mostly Afro-Cuban and Mexican dances (● Example 3.10). References to Latin and Caribbean music appear as early as in Gershwin's "Land of the Gay Caballero" from *Girl Crazy* (1930) and memorably in Cole Porter's "Begin the Beguine" from *Jubilee* (1935), where the composer uses rhythms associated with this dance from French Martinique. In his score of compelling—if not always accurate—Latin references in *West Side Story*, Bernstein makes the region's driving and repetitious rhythms work to great advantage in "America" and the "Mambo," among other numbers. Latin influences have appeared as novelties in many musicals such as the song "Conga!" in Bernstein's *Wonderful Town* (1953) and "Spanish Rose" from Charles Strouse's *Bye Bye Birdie* (1960), where it carries the designation of a "tango." Other scores with rich influences from either Iberian or Latin sources are *Man of La Mancha* (1965) and *In the Heights* (2008).

Given the large numbers of Jews who participated in the American entertainment industry during the twentieth century, it is predictable that one finds Jewish influence on the musical theater.[3] As Jack Gottlieb has demonstrated, popular songs from the first half of the twentieth century frequently resemble Jewish liturgical modes.[4] Gottlieb, however, cites associations that would escape most musicians, let alone casual listeners. More obvious Jewish references appear in shows on Jewish topics, such as *Milk and Honey* (1961) with a score by Jerry Herman, and *Fiddler on the Roof* (1964) with music by Jerry Bock. Typical musical signifiers include the harmonic minor scale, melodic augmented second, imitations of cantorial singing (such as in "If I Were a Rich Man"), and klezmer's rapid dance rhythms (such as the wedding scene of *Fiddler*).

What might be referred to as the "classic" style of theatrical songs, often described as "Tin Pan Alley"—represented in the work of Berlin, the Gershwin brothers, Rodgers and Hart, Cole Porter, Rodgers and Hammerstein, and others—reigned supreme into the 1960s. Earlier musical styles from African American musicians such as spirituals, ragtime, jazz, and blues had been assimilated easily into the musical, but waves of African American influence after World War II, including rhythm and blues, rock-and-roll, gospel, and soul, entered the theater more slowly as songwriters continued to make use of earlier styles. Shows based mostly on rock and other popular styles did not appear until the late 1960s, and use of these styles was rare by older composers. Charles Strouse (born 1928) wrote two songs with some musical signifiers of 1950s rock-and-roll for *Bye Bye Birdie* (1960), to be sung by a character based on Elvis Presley, but "Honestly Sincere" and "One Last Kiss" were novelties in an otherwise traditional score. *Hair* (1967) was the first musical that could support the moniker "rock musical," with an amplified score by Galt MacDermot based primarily on a typical rock beat played by a common rock ensemble, with obvious bass lines and a prominent backbeat. The title tune, "Easy to Be Hard," and "Aquarius" were major hits (🔊 Example 3.11). Several more shows with similarly popular scores followed soon thereafter, including Stephen Schwartz's *Godspell* and *Jesus Christ Superstar* by Andrew Lloyd Webber and Tim Rice, both from 1971. Both scores demonstrate that "rock musicals" tended to include other styles, such as a counterpoint song inspired by Irving Berlin's music in *Godspell* ("All for the Best") and a campy 1930s soft-shoe in *Jesus Christ Superstar* ("King Herod's Song").

Schwartz's *Godspell* illustrates how popular styles appeared in scores by young composers starting around 1970.[5] Schwartz (b. 1948) understood rock, Motown, and the work of singer/songwriters such as Laura Nyro, James Taylor, Joni Mitchell, and Carole King. He agreed to write a new score for the existing show in March 1971, quickly composing a dozen songs in five weeks for a May Off Broadway opening. For each tune Schwartz chose a model and wrote a tune somewhat like that, usually focusing on a song's harmonic tendencies or accompanimental pattern. "Day by Day," for example, was inspired by Burt Bacharach's "What the World Needs Now," a waltz with many seventh chords. Schwartz wanted more energy later in the repetitious tune and switched to quadruple meter and a rock beat. The model for Schwartz's "Bless the Lord" was Laura Nyro's "Save the Country," especially the piano accompaniment, her use of bass notes that are not in the chord, and tempo changes. Schwartz's model for "All Good Gifts" was "Fire and Rain" by James Taylor, with a piano accompaniment not unlike certain tunes by Elton John. "Light of the World," the first act finale, was based on "Gemini Child" by the Mamas & the Papas, which had an accompanimental pattern in quarter notes of "boom— boom—chink," with a dissonant chord on the third beat. Of the four songs considered here, this sounds the most like rock.

Rhythm and blues, rock, gospel, and soul have filled scores in musical theater since about 1970, including those for *Don't Bother Me, I Can't Cope* (1972), *The Wiz* (1975), *Your Arms Too Short to Box with God* (1976), *Bringin' da Noise, Bringin' da Funk* (1996), and other shows. These primarily African American shows by Micki Grant, Charlie Smalls, Daryl Waters, and others demonstrated that audiences craved popular music in a theatrical context. Andrew Lloyd Webber showed his ability to write in popular styles from his earliest shows (such as *Jesus Christ Superstar*), and he continued to use these styles in his huge hits *Cats* (1981) and *Phantom of the Opera* (1986). In *Cats*, for example, the rock sound of "The Rum Tum Tugger" and funky, bump-and-grind music for "Macavity: The Mystery Cat" exist alongside music reminiscent of Puccini in "Growltiger's Last Stand" and the famous power ballad "Memory." Schwartz has continued his cultivation of popular styles in *Wicked* (2003), where the character Elphaba is a pop diva, singing in a style borrowing from rhythm and blues. Jonathan Larson's score for *Rent* (1996) is a catalog of various popular styles worked seamlessly into a strong story and rendered all the more powerful by Larson's keen sense of illustrating characters through lyrics. Another use of popular styles in the theater has been the "jukebox musical," where the catalog of one songwriter or popular music group becomes the basis for a score. Major jukebox musicals have included *Mamma Mia!* (based on songs by ABBA, 2001) and *Jersey Boys* (The Four Seasons, 2005).

Rap has appeared in musical theater, such as *In the Heights* (2008), a potent combination of various Latin styles and rap with music and lyrics by Lin-Manuel Miranda. Rap appears in such songs as "96,000" and the title song (● Example 3.12). Hollywood has used rap in musicals as well, such as in *Beat Street* (1984). But the principal of rhythmicized speech was not invented for rap, and one can find examples in earlier Broadway shows, and even earlier in the patter songs of Italian comic opera or Gilbert and Sullivan operettas from the nineteenth century, but certainly not with a rap accompaniment. Meredith Willson, for example, explored the possibility in *The Music Man* (1957) in such songs as "Trouble." Willson's light patter style for Harold Hill presented the character with the requisite verbal virtuosity for a musical con man. And Stephen Sondheim, who is particularly adept at reproducing pastiche versions of earlier styles, uses patter as one element of contrapuntal songs in *Company* ("Getting Married Today," 1970) and *Pacific Overtures* ("Please Hello," 1976).

Non-Western musical styles have made occasional appearances in the theater, most prominently in Sondheim's *Pacific Overtures* and in *The Lion King* (1997). The latter, based on the 1994 animated musical film by the same name with a score by Elton John and Tim Rice, as a stage musical includes new songs that make purposeful use of African sounds, such as "One by One" by Lebo M and "Shadowland" by Hans Zimmer, Lebo M, and Mark Mancina. Perhaps following the lead of *Pacific Overtures*'s use of Japanese instruments and theatrical styles, the African musical sensibility is enriched by a wide variety of percussion instruments. Combined with director Julie Taymor's imaginative production, *The Lion King* is profoundly different from standard Broadway fare. Stephen Schwartz made use of African and Latin models in his score to *Children of Eden* (1991) in the songs "Generations" and "The Naming," but world music has not made the same splash in the musical theater that it has in the popular music industry.

MARIAN WALTZES AND HAROLD MARCHES: SONG TYPES AND CONVENTIONS

The musical styles described above constitute major influences on musical theater, but what audiences have heard also has been determined by types of songs that carry their own stylistic expectations. Below is a selective list of these types more or less in chronological order of their appearance.

In the late nineteenth century, musical theater included frequent examples of sentimental popular songs, most famous in the earlier music of Stephen Collins Foster (1826–1864). These songs had lyrical, singable melodies with touches of chromaticism, and simple harmonies. Texts tended to address home, hearth, and nostalgia. A famous use of such a song on Broadway is "After the Ball" by Charles K. Harris, a huge hit that was interpolated in *A Trip to Chinatown* (1891) and then appeared in *Show Boat* (1927) to lend credence to an event from the 1890s. Broadway composers wrote such songs as well, a famous example being "Oh Promise Me" from *Robin Hood* (1891), with a score by Reginald De Koven. The song remained a favorite for wedding ceremonies well into the twentieth century.

Sentimental parlor songs appeared from Tin Pan Alley, the New York sheet music industry. Musical theater helped popularize these songs, and there were various types in the repertory. For the first few decades of the twentieth century George M. Cohan (1878–1942), the most successful writer and director of musical comedies, was also a major writer of hits for Tin Pan Alley. His songs included two-steps like "Give My Regards to Broadway" and waltzes such as "Mary." Cohan's strongly melodic songs clearly reflected the music of his time.

The waltz was old by this time, having developed in Austria in the late eighteenth century. Its triple meter was popular in sentimental songs, including "After the Ball." If not for the waltz's growing popularity in the theater, it might have died, but Franz Lehár wrote several in his score to the immensely popular operetta *The Merry Widow* (New York première, 1907), helping to make the waltz a dominant type of theatrical song for most of the twentieth century. There are many examples of fine waltzes in the operettas of Victor Herbert, Sigmund Romberg, and Rudolf Friml, and Richard Rodgers became one of the finest waltz composers of his time, as heard in such tunes as "Out of My Dreams" from *Oklahoma!* (1947) and "Ten Minutes Ago" from *Cinderella* (1957; 🎵 Example 3.13). Sondheim's score to *A Little Night Music* (1973) is notable for its many waltzes, as well as other distinctive dance types.

The two-step became a popular dance before 1900. Among the most significant writers of two-steps was John Philip Sousa, whose marches provided dance music in social halls. Sousa also wrote for theater, and one of his marches heard on stage was "El Capitan," from the 1896 show by the same name. Marches became ubiquitous in the musical theater, heard frequently in 1920s operettas, especially in male chorus numbers like "Stouthearted Men" from Romberg's *The New Moon*

(1928). Examples of marches from later shows are "Seventy-Six Trombones" and "The Wells Fargo Wagon" from Meredith Willson's *The Music Man* (1957) and "Motherhood" and "Before the Parade Passes by" from *Hello, Dolly!* (1963).

Musical theater composers also have made use of other European dances, building upon traditions established in European operetta. Johann Strauss, for example, in operettas such as *Die Fledermaus* (1874) included polkas in rapid duple meter as well as waltzes. Richard Rodgers wrote a polka for the famous scene featuring "Shall We Dance?" in *The King and I* (1951), and the song "The Lusty Month of May" from Lerner and Loewe's *Camelot* (1960) strongly resembles a polka (◗ Example 3.14). In *Candide* (1956), Leonard Bernstein referred to several European dances, including the polka in "We Are Women," the gavotte in "Life Is Happiness" and "The Venice Gavotte" (the same melody), the schottische in "Bon Voyage," and the barcarolle in "The King's Barcarolle." The score also includes waltzes and a tango.

Another song type that appeared fairly early in the twentieth century, and probably derived from Gilbert and Sullivan,[6] was the counterpoint, or combination song, explored by Irving Berlin in a number of his scores. Such a song includes two different melodies that can be combined, meaning that they are based upon the same harmonic scheme and do not clash when sounding together. Usually the tunes are sung separately and then combined as a third verse. Berlin first did this in *Watch Your Step* with the song "Play a Simple Melody," in which he contrasted a folk-like melody such as Stephen Foster might have written with a more modern, syncopated ditty.[7] Berlin's most famous examples of counterpoint songs appear in his later musicals: "You're Just in Love" from *Call Me Madam* (1950), and "An Old-Fashioned Wedding," which Berlin wrote for the 1966 revival of *Annie Get Your Gun* (◗ Example 3.15). Other composers who have written such songs are Meredith

Willson (who combined "Will I Ever Tell You?" and "Lida Rose" in *The Music Man*) and Stephen Schwartz (who has included such a song in most of his shows, including, for example "All for the Best" in *Godspell*, 1971, and "What Is This Feeling?" in *Wicked*, 2003).

The ballad as a song type goes back many years, but by the early twentieth century in American popular music it was usually a song with a verse and a chorus in a slower tempo that included the song's melody, usually presented in a 32-bar form with 8-measure phrases in a repetitious form such as AABA or ABAC. Ballads were love songs or contemplative solo numbers, such as "Why Do I Love You?" from *Show Boat* (1927) and "Embraceable You" from *Girl Crazy* (1930), both with verses in ABAC form (● Example 3.16). "People Will Say We're in Love" from *Oklahoma!* (1943) is in AABA form, with a B section that is musically related to the A section.

A dance style from early in the twentieth century was the soft shoe, a tap dance performed with soft-soled shoes without metal taps. George Primrose popularized such steps in minstrel shows in the late nineteenth century,[8] and the soft shoe remained in the musical theater for decades. The musical style that developed to accompany such dances was a ballad-like song in quadruple meter with frequent dotted eighth-sixteenth note rhythms. One of the most famous such tunes appeared in the film *The Wizard of Oz* (1939) with the Scarecrow's "If I Only Had a Brain," soon reprised to fit the different needs of the Tin Man and Cowardly Lion. The soft-shoe has remained in the musical theater in numbers evoking earlier times, such as "Potiphar's Song" (marked in the score " 'Twenties' style") from Andrew Lloyd Webber's *Joseph and the Amazing Technicolor Dreamcoat* (1968), the Wolf's "Hello Little Girl" in Sondheim's *Into the Woods* (1987), and the Wizard's "Wonderful" in *Wicked* (2003).

Lehman Engel's designation of the rhythm song involves pieces driven forward by a propulsive beat. There have been many such songs in musical theater based on popular music since the 1960s, but Engel here refers to what might be called the classical period of Broadway through about 1960. He names as examples of rhythm songs "Luck Be a Lady" from *Guys and Dolls* (1950) and "I'm Gonna Wash That Man Right Out of My Hair" from *South Pacific* (1949), and mentions as well such composite types as the rhythm-ballad in "Tonight" (a beguine) from *West Side Story* (1957). The kind of repetitious rhythms heard in these songs is reminiscent of dances.

Strongly propulsive rhythms have also played a major role on Broadway in tap dance numbers, a popular feature of many shows since the 1920s. For such a dance, metal taps are affixed to the soles of shoes, making the dancer's feet a novelty percussion instrument that frequently "plays" solo breaks within the orchestration. The film *42nd Street* (1933) includes representative examples of tap dancing, especially by the star Ruby Keeler, from a time when many Broadway stars and choruses tapped their ways through faster dance numbers. Many of the early tap dancers were male, and among the stars who appeared on Broadway (and many film musicals as well) were Bill "Bojangles" Robinson, Fred Astaire, Gene Kelly, and the Nicholas Brothers. Examples of female stars known for their tap dancing include Marilyn Miller, Adele Astaire, Ginger Rogers, and Ann Miller. Although tap dancing became less common after World War II, it remained in shows making period references to the 1920s and 1930s, such as in the Broadway version of *42nd Street* (1980), *Crazy for You* (1992), and *The Drowsy Chaperone* (2006). *The Tap Dance Kid* (1983), *Jelly's Last Jam* (1992), and *Bring In 'da Noise, Bring in 'da Funk* (1996) were African American shows that made rich use of tap dancing. The African American tap dancer Savion Glover appeared in all three of these shows.

Musical theater composers have sometimes accessed lesser-known musical styles to serve a specific character or dramatic situation. A prominent example appears in Lerner and Loewe's *My Fair Lady* (1956), where the lower-class character Alfred P. Doolittle sings two songs based on the musical style typical of the English music halls, the British equivalent of American vaudeville: "With a Little Bit of Luck" and "Get Me to the Church on Time," rousing marches sung with texts that celebrate the interests of a working-class rogue. The subtle style of the French cabaret with its folksy melodies and common accordion accompaniment appear in various musicals, such as in "Those Canaan Days" from Lloyd Webber's *Joseph and the Amazing Technicolor Dreamcoat*, which uses a wide variety of musical types. Stephen Schwartz also used the French cabaret sound, associated closely with Edith Piaf, in his *The Baker's Wife* (1976), especially in the opening "Chanson."

Other song types common in musicals imply function rather than a specific musical style. Lehman Engel describes three such types. The musical scene is a segment of a show or film with nearly continuous singing and perhaps dialogue with underscoring, usually through contrasting musical styles, where the plot advances and the audience learns something about the characters. Examples of musical scenes include "Where's the Mate for Me?"/"Make Believe" from *Show Boat* (where the main love interests Magnolia and Gaylord meet), "If I Loved You" from *Carousel* (another meeting for the principal couple), the opening of Sondheim's *Sunday in the Park with George* (1984, where the audience meets all of the main characters and situations), and "Dancing through Life" from *Wicked* (where much of the plot is developed). The comedy song fulfills an important function in the musical. Engel distinguishes between short and long joke songs, the definitions of which depend upon how long it takes to develop each humorous moment. "Anything You Can Do" from *Annie Get Your Gun* (1946) is a short joke song, and "The True Love of My Life" from *Brigadoon* (1947) is an effective long joke song. Engel's charm song is a self-defining designation, an opportunity for a character to seduce the audience. The type often appears as an "I want" song, sung near the beginning of a show with a main character revealing his or her desires. Examples include "Something's Coming" from *West Side Story* and "Wouldn't It Be Loverly" from *My Fair Lady*.

Musical style is a powerful tool in conveying a show's dramatic sense. When working on *The Music Man*, composer, lyricist, and book writer Meredith Willson came up with a tune that worked both as a march and waltz, and he made use of the possibility when describing his main characters musically. Marian Paroo and Harold Hill are associated by singing the same melody, but he shows his masculinity and salesmanship by singing his march "Seventy-Six Trombones" (◐ Example 3.17). Marian's version is the more feminine waltz of "Goodnight, My Someone" (◐ Example 3.18). In the second act, after Hill has started to consider his feelings for Marian, they alternate between the two versions of the tune, and Hill confirms his love for Marian when he sings her version, a telling moment made possible by the differences in musical style between the march and waltz. When we fall in love we may not march or waltz, but we certainly expect a show's creators to impart some of the dramatic meaning in a show through their use of musical style.

NOTES

1. Lehmann Engel, *American Musical Theater* (New York: Macmillan, 1975), pp. 77–131.
2. See Raymond Knapp, *The American Musical and the Formation of National Identity* (Princeton, NJ: Princeton University Press, 2005), pp. 191–92.
3. For a useful study of Jews in the musical theater, see Andrea Most, *Making Americans: Jews and the Broadway Musical* (Cambridge, MA: Harvard University Press, 2004).

4. See Jack Gottlieb, *Funny, It Doesn't Sound Jewish: How Yiddish Songs and Synagogue Melodies Influenced Tin Pan Alley, Broadway, and Hollywood* (Albany: State University of New York in association with the Library of Congress, 2004).

5. For consideration of Schwartz's music from *Godspell*, see Paul R. Laird, *The Musical Theater of Stephen Schwartz: From* Godspell *to* Wicked *and Beyond* (Lanham, MD: Rowman and Littlefield, 2014), pp. 19–24 and 29–39.

6. Raymond Knapp, "'How great thy charm, thy sway how excellent!' Tracing Gilbert and Sullivan's Legacy in the American Musical," in *The Cambridge Companion to Gilbert and Sullivan* (Cambridge: Cambridge University Press, 2009), pp. 102–215.

7. Laurence Bergeen, *As Thousands Cheer: The Life of Irving Berlin* (New York: Viking, 1990), pp. 106–7.

8. See Mark Knowles, *Tap Roots: The Early History of Tap Dancing* (Jefferson, NC: McFarland, 2002), pp. 108–9.

4

Evolution of Dance in the Golden Age of the American "Book Musical"

LIZA GENNARO

■ ◻ ■

DURING THE "GOLDEN AGE" OF the American musical, generally identified as the period between 1943 and 1964, dance functioned as an essential narrative tool in musical theater production. Choreographers, partnering with writers, composers, and lyricists, developed a collaborative creative approach in which dance, music, and spoken narrative combined to produce the "book musical," an "integrated" form in which song and dance emerge seamlessly from spoken dialogue. Creating dances for a "book musical" requires a method different from that of concert venues, where the initial formative impulse of a dance develops solely from the mind of the choreographer. The musical theater choreographer's assignment is to negotiate and absorb the precepts defined by the time, place, and setting of the libretto, along with directorial choices regarding performance style and physical elements of the production, and to discover how those elements translate into dance. It is within the context of the "book musical"—and not in relation to so-called dansicals such as *Cats* (1982), *Contact* (2000), and *Movin' Out* (2002), which are more closely associated with the artistic process of the concert-venue choreographer—that I will discuss the evolution of dance in musicals.

From this perspective, the Golden Age began with Rodgers and Hammerstein's *Oklahoma!* (1943), choreography by Agnes de Mille, and ended with Bock and Harnick's *Fiddler on the Roof* (1964), directed and choreographed by Jerome Robbins. During these years, de Mille and Robbins set the standard for making dances in the "book musical," and while their methods were markedly different, they established a template that was adopted by future generations. In order to gauge the impact of de Mille's and Robbins's innovations, it is important to understand the function of dance in the musical theater prior to *Oklahoma!*

In the 1920s and '30s, dances in Broadway musicals served as fanciful interruptions to often-whimsical plots. Dance directors of the period were highly skilled professionals who created clever, amusing, and extravagant dance sequences capable of evoking immediate visceral audience response. One of the most notable and successful of the early twentieth-century dance directors was Ned Wayburn, who staged more than 600 revues and musical comedies on Broadway and who codified a system of choreography and maintained a popular chain of dancing schools that trained young hopefuls to dance in Broadway choruses.[1]

Wayburn's technique was rooted in American Delsarte, military drills, and the hierarchical systems of nineteenth-century ballet spectacles. His strategy for success was a methodically prescribed system for making dances that included six categories of musical theater dancing: Musical Comedy Technique, Toe Specialties, Exhibition Ballroom, Acrobatic Work, Tapping and Stepping, and Modern Americanized

Ballet (Statyner, 8). In his book, *The Art of Stage Dancing*, he reveals an exact approach to making dances:

> The average routine consists of ten steps, one to bring you onto the stage, which is called a traveling step, eight steps to the dance proper, usually set to about 64 bars of music or the length of two choruses of a popular song; and an exit step, which is a special step designed to form a climax to the dance and provoke the applause as you go off the stage. [2]

Unpretentious and clear-thinking, Wayburn drilled his choruses on straightness of lines, body angle, and kick height, and aspired to an aesthetic of clean, glossy polish that smacked audiences into alertness. His brand of surefire dance entertainment dominated the Broadway scene in the 1920s where he and other dance directors (including George White, John Tiller, Bobby Connolly, Sammy Lee, and Albertina Rasch) enjoyed success.

It was important among this coterie of dance directors to develop individual signature styles. Rasch, one of the few women in the field, was a veteran of vaudeville, Broadway revues, and musicals. Born in Vienna in 1891, she trained at the Imperial Ballet School and performed with the Viennese Opera before traveling to America, where she enjoyed a successful career as a performer dancing at the New York Hippodrome and touring her act, a "traditional pointe specialty," in vaudeville (Reis 1983, 95). In the early 1920s Rasch joined the production staff of the Keith-Orpheum circuit, where she created the Albertina Rasch Dancers. Her lines of girls were unique in that they did not employ the tap and musical comedy dance vocabularies that were de rigueur during the period. Rather, Rasch created dances using classical *port de bras* and *pointe* technique, danced to American jazz. Her husband and musical director Dimitri Tiomkin reported that she "liked the idea of adapting the toe dancing technique of the ballet to the slangy rhythms of jazz. It appealed to her interest in novelties of choreography" (▶ Example 4.1).[3]

Indeed, novelty was a hallmark of the period and one of the defining elements of the vaudeville, musical, and revue genres. Performers and dance directors, working tirelessly to invent performance acts that showcased unique talents and distinguished them from competitors, borrowed movement vocabularies from a wide range of dance styles. One of the most pillaged dance sources was African American vernacular dance, appropriated by white performers and absorbed into American performance culture.[4] In the twentieth century, legions of African American dance makers remained uncredited and poorly compensated for their creative contributions to the genre. However, despite the difficulties that plagued them in their attempts at recognition, they continued to create performance opportunities for themselves.

Throughout the 1910s, black musicals, which had enjoyed success in the first decade of the twentieth century with productions starring Bert Williams and George Walker, were absent from Broadway. During those years they quietly developed in theaters away from Broadway; and in 1921 the groundbreaking musical *Shuffle Along*, written by Noble Sissle and Eubie Blake and starring Aubrey Lyles and Flournoy Miller, opened at New York's 63rd Street Theatre.[5] The show was an enormous hit and introduced a new kind of dance to the musical theater, as noted by Marshall and Jean Stearns: "The most impressive innovation of *Shuffle Along* was the dancing of the sixteen girl chorus line . . . above all, musical comedy took on a new and rhythmic life, and chorus girls began learning to dance to jazz."[6]

As jazz entered the musical theater dance lexicon, so too did the earliest examples of American modern dance. A notable contributor to the evolution of musical theater dance in the 1920s was John Murray Anderson, who began his career as an exhibition ballroom dancer and produced the *Greenwich*

Village Follies, which featured the "ballet ballads," narrative tales that combined song and dance into a cohesive whole.[7] Anderson demonstrated a sophisticated dance palette when, for his 1923 ballet ballad "The Garden of Kama," he featured a young dancer named Martha Graham, before her breakthrough as one of the greatest modern dancers of the twentieth century (Anderson, 81). In 1925 Anderson engaged Graham again, this time under the direction of Michio Ito.[8]

Anderson was among the first to demonstrate a taste for nonconventional casting, not only among his principal performers but also in his choruses, by deliberately choosing dancers and showgirls who were not "off the production line" but rather were individual "types" (Anderson, 62). Seymour Felix, another proponent of the individuated chorus, was among the earliest dance directors to consider the notion of integrated dance. In 1926 he bemoaned the standard chorus girl number packed with kicks and tricks that in his words "became a colorful but negative interruption to the action or comedy of the musical comedy book" and in 1928 proclaimed, "No longer are routines a matter of speed and noise . . . the cycle of acrobatics, 'hot' dancing, and stomping is over. . . . Scrambled legs have become a bore. The important thing today is the so called 'book number.'"[9] It is remarkable that Felix spoke in terms of the "book number" as early as 1928; however, despite his protestations he—like other dance directors including Sammy Lee, who created the dances for Hammerstein and Kern's landmark musical *Show Boat* (1927)—did not cause a systemic overhaul in musical theater dance production.

While *Show Boat* is lauded in terms of musical theater writing, its dances have barely been considered. A 1928 review from the *American* offers some indication of them:

> Norma Terris (Magnolia) does a beautiful insinuating skirt dance with all the glorified girls as a background, Captain Andy does a humorous two-step with Parthy Ann, and Sammy White

performs an extraordinary clog eccentric dance. Then, too, there
are, in addition to these numbers, the extraordinary clogs, tap
dances, waltzes and even can-can. [10]

The numbers were clearly craft-worthy and entertaining, but
they employed standard musical theater dance vocabularies.
While Hammerstein and Kern succeeded in creating a groundbreaking work in terms of integration of song and text, Lee
created well-crafted dances that were unremarkable in terms
of innovation.

George Balanchine is credited with reenvisioning dance in
musicals and employing dance as an integral element essential to plot development, with his choreography for Rodgers
and Hart's *On Your Toes* (1936). His ballet "Slaughter on
Tenth Avenue," which starred Tamara Geva and Ray Bolger,
was essential to the advancement of the musical play, which
depended upon its storytelling capabilities (▶ Example 4.2).
Between 1936 and 1951, Balanchine choreographed over fif-
teen Broadway shows and introduced a highly sophisticated,
classically based choreography to the genre. For Rodgers and
Hart's *Boys from Syracuse* (1938) he created an *Adagio* for principal dancers George Church, Heidi Vossler, and Betty Bruce
that represented the internal struggle of a man in love with two
women. The women's sexuality was illustrated in their dance
vocabularies; Vossler dancing *en pointe* represented "the del-
icacy of conjugal love" while Bruce in tap shoes represented
a "steamier . . . carnal" attraction.[11] Photographs of the dance
show complex intertwining of the three bodies reminiscent of
Balanchine's 1928 ballet *Apollo* and demonstrate a high level
of choreographic invention (see Figure 4.1). However, despite
his undisputed choreographic gifts, Balanchine in the 1930s
was working in a genre that, in terms of dance, was subject to
the prevalent dance styles of the period. While he was able to
create moments of innovative dance, he was also required to

(a)

(b)

FIGURE 4.1a and 4.1b Photographs from *Boys from Syracuse* and *Apollo*. George Balanchine's *Apollo*, created in 1928, pictured in revival here for New York City Ballet with Jacques d'Amboise, Melissa Hayden, Maria Tallchief, and Patricia Wilde (Martha Swope photographer, used by permission), demonstrates the complex intertwinings of bodies that Balanchine favored in his ballet choreography, which can also be seen in the photo of his choreography from *Boys from Syracuse* (1938), featuring George Church, Heidi Vossler, and Betty Bruce. These photographs demonstrate the high level of invention and craft typical of Balanchine in both his concert and Broadway choreographies. (Photographs reproduced with permission of the Jerome Robbins Dance Division, The New York Public Library for the Performing Arts, Astor, Lenox and Tilden Foundations) employ acrobatics, novelty dance, tap (designed by a talented group of uncredited African American choreographers including Herbie Harper [*On Your Toes*] and Billy Pierce [*Babes in Arms*, 1937]).[12]

In his Broadway shows Balanchine adhered to a European aesthetic of glamour and exoticism evident in photographs of the *pas de trois* from *Boys from Syracuse*, which depicts his ballerinas in transparent harem pants and bare midriffs. Fantasy and parody were standard features of his integrated narrative ballets, as for example in "Honeymoon Ballet" from *I Married an Angel* (1938), which featured a corps de ballet, *en pointe*, dressed as airplanes with wings on their arms and aviator helmets, and "Peter's Journey" from *Babes in Arms* (1937) in which dancers portrayed mermaids *en pointe* in an underwater ballet (Hill, 2). His dances were unquestionably of high quality but did not cause radical alteration in the production of dance in musicals. That would not occur until 1943 with Agnes de Mille's dances for *Oklahoma!*

Hired based on the monumental success of her ballet *Rodeo* (1942) created for the *Ballet Russe de Monte Carlo*, de Mille, representing regular American folk with her dancing cowboys and prairie girls, brought an idealized image of the American West to the commercial theater, and with the support of Rodgers, Hammerstein, and director Rouben Mamoulian, created a set of dances that related directly to the time and setting of the libretto and enhanced character development. Unlike her previous Broadway experiences, Howard Deitz and Arthur Schwartz's *Flying Colors* (1932) and Harold Arlen and E. Y. Harburg's *Hooray for What* (1937), for *Oklahoma!* de Mille was given the opportunity to invent a movement lexicon that inhabited the entire show from beginning to end. Employing techniques she developed as a self-producing soloist in the 1920s and '30s, when she created and performed dance characterizations rendered in ballet and pantomime, and incorporating lessons learned from Martha Graham and Louis Horst, a composer and one of the primary architects of American modern dance, de Mille developed a system for expressing ideas through dance in the "book musical."

Based on Lynn Riggs's 1931 play *Green Grow the Lilacs, Oklahoma!* tells the story of three main characters: Laurey, a young plainswoman; Curly, a cowboy; and Jud, Laurey's farmhand and the play's villain. Laurey and Curly are in love; however, neither will admit to the attraction. Jud is attracted to Laurey, but she is terrified of him. The action of the play revolves around Laurey's decision to attend a box social with Jud, in part to spite Curly. As de Mille focused on the relationships between the three principal characters and Laurey's curiosity about the collection of sexually titillating postcards displayed on the walls of Jud's cabin, it was her conceit that Laurey secretly identified with the girls on the postcards and that she was as frightened of her own desires as she was of Jud.[13] She conceived the ballet "Laurey Makes Up Her Mind" as a dream exploring Laurey's attraction to both Curly and Jud, manifest in what becomes a nightmare exploring her repressed desires.

In the ballet, Laurey and Curly wed, but as Curly lifts Laurey's veil she sees to her horror that she has married Jud. Ignoring her pleas for help, the wedding guests and Curly fade into the distance. Laurey flees only to discover herself in a saloon where she is confronted and taunted by the Postcard Girls—garishly dressed saloon dancers. Employing early modern dance techniques of distortion, and Louis Horst's method of Introspection-Expression, de Mille distills the Postcard Girls' movement down to the merest suggestion of a Wild West saloon exhibition (⏺ Example 4.3).[14] The movements are rooted in the can-can and twentieth-century burlesque movement lexicons, both appropriate to the period, but rather than succumbing to pastiche, de Mille uses the vocabularies as a basis for movement innovation. Representing

Laurey's innocent imaginings of wanton women, the Postcard Girls perform in slow motion. Their faces are hard and frozen and they roll their shoulders as if trying to escape an ill-fitting blouse. Drooping like rag dolls when lifted by the men, they appear flaccid and impotent. Devoid of energy, humanity, and sexuality, they move mechanically through their deconstructed can-can. By engaging in a modernistic deconstruction of the archetypal dance hall girl, de Mille rebuilt the construct as an extension of Laurey's psyche.

The ballet is one example of de Mille's highly sophisticated, multilayered system for creating dances in the musical theater and demonstrates her ability to employ modernist methods of movement innovation in a manner that Broadway audiences could absorb. Trusting in the potential of dance to serve as a conduit for emotions and ideas, de Mille created multilayered constructs in the musical theater that were grounded in the time, place, and characters of the libretto. Rife with social and political implications, de Mille's dances expanded the parameters of the libretto and disrupted the Broadway casting blueprint by knocking the iconic chorus girl, a patriarchal fabrication of female beauty and allure, off her pedestal; chorus girls were replaced with women whose appearances were ordinary, but whose ability to express emotion through movement was extraordinary. In a little over a year, de Mille caused an ideological shift in the function of dance on Broadway and opened a portal on a fertile creative landscape.

The most significant arrival to Broadway, post-de Mille, was Jerome Robbins, who choreographed *On the Town* (1944), based on his ballet *Fancy Free* (1944). Robbins would become de Mille's staunchest competition and would with her define the production of musical theater dance in the "book musical." In his first two shows, *On the Town*, and *Billion Dollar Baby* (1945), de Mille's influence is apparent in the psychological ballets he created, but a greater influence on his work would be revealed in his strict adherence to accurate depictions of time, place, and character—lessons he learned as a member of Gluck Sandor's Dance Center.[15] Sandor, a choreographer for the Group Theater, an American acting company inspired by the work of the Russian director Constantin Stanislavsky, employed actors and directors from the Group to instruct his troupe of dancers on contemporary acting techniques. Robbins remembered his time in Sandor's company saying, "We never did anything on stage without knowing who we were, where we were, & why."[16]

Committed to the ideas of time and place in relation to character, Robbins, first relying on Stanislavsky and later employing Method Acting techniques learned at Lee Strasberg's Actors Studio, engaged in painstakingly extensive research whenever he embarked on a new musical theater project. Explaining his choreographic process for *Billion Dollar Baby*, set in 1920s New York, Robbins told *New York Post* reporter Harriet Johnson,

> I studied all the cartoons of the period I could lay my hands on. I went to the Museum of Modern Art and looked at all the possible movies of the 20s. I talked to everyone who remembered the period to find out what people were, thought, felt, said, and did. I wanted my dances to portray the kind of people who were typical of the time. [17]

By basing his choreographic inventions on authentic sources, Robbins supplied himself with made-to-order movement vocabularies to set within the dramatic structures of his dance numbers (◉ Example 4.4).

For his ballet "Small House of Uncle Thomas" from Rodgers and Hammerstein's *The King and I* (1951), Robbins engaged Cambodian dance scholar Mara Von Sellheim to assist him in creating dances for the show (Jowitt, 181). Film recordings of Von Sellheim's company demonstrate how closely Robbins followed her instruction in terms of movement vocabulary and costuming, but it was Robbins's ability to infuse the movement with an American musical comedy sensibility that makes the dance a success in the framework of the show. By developing comic moments, for example, when the ballet's heroine, Eliza, reaches the icy river and is met by an angel who escorts her across the ice by way of a charming duet that fuses images from Frederick Ashton's *Les Patineurs* (1937) with Cambodian dance to create a delightfully humorous movement interlude, Robbins provided Broadway audiences with an entry point into his excursion into Cambodian dance and made the ballet accessible and entertaining in a musical theater context (● Example 4.5).

As his musical theater career progressed, Robbins became increasingly invested in dances that made logical sense, supported dramatic intent, and provided a stylistic continuum from the libretto. With the exception of *West Side Story* (1957), which stands as an anomaly in Robbins's musical theater career (see below), Robbins had a chameleon-like ability to absorb dance styles so completely that his own particular movement style was obscured. As his success grew, so too did his frustrations with the lack of control afforded choreographers in the musical theater, which operates as a hierarchical system in which the director and writers occupy the upper rungs of the ladder and choreographers the lower. It was a condition he sought to alter with *Look Ma I'm Dancin'* (1948), a parody of his days touring with Ballet Theater, which he wrote and co-directed with George Abbott. Serving twice as co-director to Abbott before his solo directorial debut with *Peter Pan* (1954), Robbins became the first in the modern line of director-choreographers, a group that also would include Bob Fosse, Gower Champion, and Michael Bennett. As Robbins's power and control increased, so too did his method of weaving dance into the fabric of the librettos.

In Jule Styne and Stephen Sondheim's *Gypsy*, a musical based on the memoir of Gypsy Rose Lee, Robbins was faced with the task of creating dances for a vaudeville child act. Rather than simply creating dances that would be appropriate to the period and genre, Robbins gave himself the additional task of constructing the musical numbers as if they had been created by Gypsy's overbearing mother Rose (Jowitt, 319). The task provided Robbins with a choreographic method to support his central tenet, that "movement is always dictated by character, situation and material."[18] The result was two brilliantly witty vaudeville numbers, depicting a cloyingly cute child star, Baby June, backed by a ragtag group of boys that included her sister Louise (the future Gypsy Rose Lee) dressed as a boy. Although the numbers feature the pampered Baby June, they also tell the story of Louise, disguised and out of step, dismissed by her mother as no more than a tagalong burden. As examples of dance, the numbers are unremarkable, but within the context of the show they serve as searing illustrations of Rose's ambition and narcissism (Example 4.6).

In 1964, with the exception of revivals and *Jerome Robbins' Broadway*, a retrospective of his choreography in musicals (1989), Robbins embarked on his last book musical for Broadway, *Fiddler on the Roof*. "The Bottle Dance," which occurs at a wedding celebration, imitates a traditional Jewish wedding custom in which guests are obligated to entertain the bride and spontaneously perform tricks, comedy routines, and acrobatics for her pleasure.[19] Robbins witnessed this custom at a Hasidic wedding ceremony in New York in which a Jewish comedian did a dance with a bottle on his head.[20] Expanding the moment to involve a group of men overtaking the celebration, Robbins created a brilliant dance that emerges seamlessly from the dramatic action and appears improvised by the characters. It represents the ideal manifestation of Robbins's legacy in the musical theater genre and serves as a model for his integrated brand of musical theater choreography (⊙ Example 4.7).

West Side Story (1957), created with Leonard Bernstein, Arthur Laurents (book), Stephen Sondheim (lyrics), and co-choreographer Peter Gennaro, stands as an aberration in Robbins's musical theater career because the dances, while adhering to Robbins's requirements in terms of time, place, and period, were also examples of movement innovation in a modernistic sense. By his own admission, Robbins, who concurrent to his Broadway career maintained an active career in the field of classical ballet, worked differently in the musical theater than he did when creating a ballet, a fact that he hoped to amend with *West Side Story*. In a Dramatist Guild symposium almost thirty years after *West Side Story*'s creation, Robbins explained what he, Leonard Bernstein, and Arthur Laurents were trying to accomplish with the show:

> I wanted to find out at that time how far we three, as "long-haired artists," . . . could go on bringing our crafts and talents to a musical. Why did we have to do it separately and elsewhere? Why did Lenny have to write an opera, Arthur a play, me a ballet? Why couldn't we, in aspiration, try to bring our deepest talents together to the commercial theater in this work? That was the true gesture of the show. (Jowitt, 266)

Robbins's fusion of ballet, jazz, and 1950s social dance idioms (see Figures 4.2 and 4.3) was so astonishing in terms of dance that after the opening of *West Side Story* he formed a new company, Ballets: U.S.A., and continued to develop *West Side Story*'s movement vocabulary for the concert stage (Jowitt, 293).[21] In terms of musical theater dance, *West Side Story* was the first and last of its kind to be created by Robbins (⊙ Example 4.8).

The generation of choreographers spawned by de Mille and Robbins, including Jack Cole, Michael Kidd, Bob Fosse,

FIGURE 4.2 *N.Y. Export: Opus Jazz* (1958), created for Jerome Robbins's company Ballets: U.S.A., further developed the movement ideas he formulated in his choreography for the "Jets" in *West Side Story* (1957). (Photograph reproduced with permission of the Jerome Robbins Dance Division, The New York Public Library for the Performing Arts, Astor, Lenox and Tilden Foundations)

Peter Gennaro, and Gower Champion, used the methodologies established by the form's ostensible parents as a template on which to base their own unique choreographic systems. Cole defined a jazz dance vocabulary for musicals with his fusion of Bharata Natyam, African American vernacular dance, and Latin forms.[22] Writing for the *New York Times* in 1948, John Martin expounded on Cole's technique,

> Cole fits into no easy category. He is not of the ballet, yet the technique he has established is probably the strictest and most spectacular anywhere to be found. He is not an orthodox "modern" dancer, for though his movement is extremely individual, it employs a great deal of objective material—from the Orient, from the Caribbean, from Harlem. Certainly, however, he is not an eclectic, for the influences that he has invoked have been completely absorbed into his own motor idiom. [23]

FIGURE 4.3 In contrast to the photograph of Jerome Robbin's *N.Y. Export: Opus Jazz*, this photograph from the film adaptation of *West Side Story* (1961) demonstrates a less formalized and more dramaturgically organic use of the movement idioms Robbins elaborated on and continued to explore in his Ballets: U.S.A. (Photograph reproduced with permission of the Billy Rose Theatre Division, The New York Public Library for the Performing Arts, Astor, Lenox and Tilden Foundations)

Engaging in extensive movement research, Cole was known to travel to remote locations in order to develop authentic dances.[24] However, despite his best intentions, it is difficult to reconcile his pursuance of dance authenticity with the fact that for *Kismet* (1953), which is set in ancient Arabia, he employed his particular fusion of swing music and Bharata Natyam, ignoring both the period and setting of the musical play (⏺ Example 4.9).

The tension between a drive toward authenticity and a disregard for it at the same time is a central element in musical theater dance creation. Negotiating that tension is one area in which the musical theater choreographer demonstrates artistic vision and creative choice. Whereas Robbins grounded his dances within the boundaries established by the libretto, Cole, with his *Kismet* dances, disregarded the time and place of the libretto, drawing from a movement lexicon that did not, in terms of authenticity, relate to the musical play. His choreography is the embodiment of what music critic Irving Kolodin called "the fruitful anachronism and the relevant absurdity."[25] And it was in the anachronistic and absurd facts of Cole's work that his choreographic voice emerged.

Cole was not the first in this generation to choreograph anachronistically. De Mille, for E. Y. Harburg and Harold Arlen's *Bloomer Girl* (1944), created "The Civil War Ballet" using American country-dance vocabulary and formations as the basis for her movement invention. The choice is notable since by the 1860s country-dance in America had been replaced by the polka, the mazurka, and the waltz as popular social dances.[26] Why then did de Mille choose the historically inaccurate American country-dance? As described by Kate Van Winkle Keller and Genevieve Shimer, country-dance is

> a group dance in which there is interaction between two or more couples and it is a democratic dance in that the couples often change positions in the set and take turns leading the figures. Only in a culture in which the absolute power of the king had been tempered by the demands of democracy could such a dance form flourish.[27]

De Mille was clearly less interested in historical authenticity than in creating a metaphoric dance language evoking democratic ideals. Creating the ballet in the final days of World War II, de Mille was intent on making a dance that offered her audience a cathartic expression of hope and renewal, rather

than an accurate depiction of the social dance of the period
(● Example 4.10).

Another important choreographic voice in the Golden Age
was Michael Kidd, who began his career as a dancer and choreographer in the early days of American ballet, working with
Eugene Loring's Dance Players and Ballet Theatre. Transferring
his talents to the commercial genre, Kidd created robust, vigorous dances that required highly trained ballet and modern
dancers willing to perform choreography demanding strong
resilient bodies. His men portrayed a sort of hypermasculinity
wielding axes in "I'm a Lonesome Polecat" from the film *Seven
Brides for Seven Brothers* (1954), and whips in the "Whip Dance"
from *Destry Rides Again* (1959). "Runyonland" and "Havana"
in *Guys and Dolls* (1950) maintained narrative through lines
while sending out strands of danced scenarios, adding idiosyncratic texture in movement and layering mood, tenor, and character. Like Robbins he was able to create dance in a wide range
of movement styles, but unlike Robbins his dances always bore
his particular movement style, characterized by high knees and
chest, impish perkiness, spectacular lifts, and muscular athlet-
icism (● Example 4.11; ● Example 4.12; ● Example 4.13).

Bob Fosse, who bridged the Golden Age and the post-
Golden Age periods, had the most powerful influence upon
the dance zeitgeist of the late twentieth century. He was inspired by Fred Astaire's classic song-and-dance-man flair,
Jack Cole's idiosyncratic use of jazz dance lexicons, de Mille's
drive toward movement innovation, and Robbins's ability to
engage song, dance, and text within a cohesive whole. In a career that began with "Steam Heat" from *Pajama Game* (1954;
● Example 4.14)—an exciting reenvisioning of a movement
lexicon popularized by, among others, vaudevillian Joe
Frisco—Fosse developed one of the most imitated movement
styles in musical theater dance, in particular with the
erotic renderings of women, presented in *Pippin* (1972) and

Chicago (1975). Fosse's obsession with overt sexual images and the objectification of women found an audience in the musical theater as his career ascent coincided with the 1960s sexual revolution. The theater community that in 1957 rejected his "Red Light Ballet" from the musical *New Girl in Town* (see Figure 4.4), an explicit romp through a nineteenth-century bordello featuring Gwen Verdon, applauded the slithering and writhing of his female chorus in *Chicago*.[28]

One of his most innovative choreographic moments occurred in *Sweet Charity* (1966) with the musical number "Big Spender" in which a group of worn-out dance hall girls tries to entice a patron to purchase a dance. Closely resembling

FIGURE 4.4 This photograph of "The Red Light Ballet" from *New Girl in Town* (1957) features Gwen Verdon atop a chair and a chorus of women in poses demonstrating Fosse's early fascination with placing the female body in overtly sexual positions, a characteristic that became a signature feature of his work. (Photograph reproduced with permission of the Billy Rose Theatre Division, The New York Public Library for the Performing Arts, Astor, Lenox and Tilden Foundations)

the quality and intent behind both de Mille's "Postcard Girls" and Antony Tudor's "has-been" goddesses in *Judgment of Paris* (1938), Fosse succeeded in creating a minimalistic, narrative dance with a literal chorus line of women who, posing side by side, move in a kind of trance punctuated with pointed isolation. Rife with innuendo, his dancers project insolent disdain and demonstrate a purely original choreographic voice. The musical theater has yet to recover from Fosse's persistent influence on choreographers and his seeming ownership of the musical theater jazz dance lexicon (▶ Example 4.15).

Peter Gennaro also bridged the period during and after the Golden Age. As a performer he danced in the chorus of *Guys and Dolls*; shared the stage with Carol Haney and Buzz Miller in "Steam Heat"; and originated the role of Carl in *Bells Are Ringing* (1956; choreography Jerome Robbins and Bob Fosse), dancing "Mu Cha Cha" with Judy Holliday. Robbins was so impressed by Gennaro's mastery of Latin dance forms, techniques learned as a student at the Katherine Dunham School of Arts and Research, that he asked him to co-choreograph *West Side Story* and assigned him the task of creating the dances for "the Sharks." Gennaro's success was based on an exuberant dance style characterized by fast footwork, isolation, and complex rhythms. Like Robbins's dances in *Fiddler on the Roof*, Gennaro's work possessed the quality of improvisation, as if the characters were acting on a spontaneous urge to dance.

Gower Champion began his theatrical career as a tap and ballroom dancer and gained popular success in the 1940s and '50s in Hollywood and on television with his wife and ballroom dance partner Marge, nee Belcher.[29] Their danced narratives portrayed the postwar desire for a return to normalcy and the reestablishment of male dominance in the workforce and at home, promoting the heteronormative ideology of the 1950s (▶ Example 4.16). As a Broadway director and choreographer, Champion introduced a cinematic sensibility to the musical theater stage by employing "continuous choreographed staging," a transitional device first used by Robbins in *West Side Story* (Gilvey). The device allowed for a seamless flow from scene to scene replacing blackouts and "in one" numbers (scenes or musical numbers performed downstage of the first wing in front of a painted drop or curtain) which enabled set changes to occur upstage. "In ones" were discontinued as soon as technology caught up with the imagination of theater artists who craved fluid transitions between scenes. Champion's further use of dance as a scenic element was evident in the opening of *Hello, Dolly!* (1962) for which he created an 1890s New York City street scene by developing a movement style based on period photographs. When interspersed with song and dialogue, this style served as a frame establishing a sense of place and style for the production. Champion used dance as a catalyst for ushering in a new era of musical theater production that sought to disguise old-fashioned stage mechanizations.

In the decades following 1964, the most common end point of the Golden Age, Broadway creators preferred reality-based dance and Robbins's late-career method of dance at the service of the libretto to de Mille's method of inserting multilayered, daedal dance structures. Consequently, dance in the "book musical" was increasingly employed in realistic terms, as in *A Chorus Line* (1975; director-choreographer Michael Bennett, co-choreographer Bob Avian), in which dancers and dance propel the story; backstage musicals such as *Dreamgirls* (1981; director-choreographer Michael Bennett, co-choreographer Michael Peters); and *42nd Street* (1980; director-choreographer Gower Champion); and theatrically stylized productions such as *Once on This Island* (1990; director-choreographer Graciela Daniele), in which dance plays a primary role in the overall gestalt of the presentation.

The 2006–07 Broadway season witnessed a change in this trend with the advent of Bill T. Jones's Tony Award–winning choreography for *Spring Awakening*, based on the play of the same title by Frank Wedekind (1891), which condemns the hypocrisy of oppressive nineteenth-century attitudes toward the body and sexuality. The writers of *Spring Awakening*, Steven Sater and Duncan Shiek, along with director Michael Mayer and Jones, freed themselves from the confining precepts of musical theater production by ignoring the historical setting of the play in terms of movement, music, and language. The production design is drawn from the period, but not authentic to it, and the music and performance style, complete with hand held microphones, borrows from a rock-concert aesthetic. Despite the absence of trained dancers, Jones used dance innovatively to express sexuality, repression, longing, and anger.

Creating a movement theme that underlines the sexual repression of the play's characters, Jones establishes a set of choreographed gestures to which he returns throughout the show. In a conversation with the author, he explained how studying Wedekind's original text and experiencing the "absurdity and symbolism" of the play gave him the courage to approach his work

> in the experience of the expressionists, [as] something that would be at once psychological and literal, that could be used like a decor that changes. . . . I was trying to understand how to set up a field of gestural movement that could track through the bulk of the piece and could be in counterpoint to the heavy psychology of the writing and the rock-and-roll nature of the music . . . the gestures were a challenge between that which is literal and that which is abstract . . . that was the biggest contribution that I made. [30]

Jones's approach to dance and movement, with its tension between the literal and the abstract, echoes de Mille's complex structures and her core belief that dance as an essentially abstract form could interact with literal narrative, thereby providing a unique layering of kinetic expression in innovative dance movement (a belief that Robbins ultimately abandoned for a more realistically integrated use of dance in musicals).

The 2007–08 season saw yet another innovative use of dance in the Tony Award–winning choreography for *In the Heights* created by choreographer Andy Blankenbuehler. Blankenbuehler allows the setting of the show, Washington Heights in New York City, a predominantly Latino (both Dominican and Puerto Rican) neighborhood in which dance is an important aspect of the culture, to permit dance to flow into the streets as both a scenic element (pedestrians moving fluidly through their day) and as spontaneously erupting dance numbers. Blankenbuehler's hook is the prevalence of dance in Latino culture, and although people do not regularly dance their way through city streets, within the context of a musical, such activity seems plausible. His fusion of hip-hop and break dance movement lexicons, both improvisatory in nature, with a formalized Broadway aesthetic, result in a joyously innovative fusion.

These examples demonstrate how the "book musical" offers choreographers a creative dance venue separate from the concert arena and requires skills often outside the realm of dance makers, including storytelling ability; character-specific movement development; ability to communicate with actors and nondancers—all while maintaining an adaptable working style that places the overall success of the show above the individual success of the choreography. The Golden Age choreographers established paradigms for choreographing the "book musical," and each subsequent generation of musical theater choreographers, cognizant of his or her predecessors' contributions to the genre, has enlivened the form with contemporary dance lexicons and theatrical strategies. Like all art, the form is in a constant state of invention and evolution.

What makes musical theater challenging as an art form is that box-office receipts measure success, which can inhibit artists' innovative impulses. It is to the credit of musical theater choreographers that they continue to reinvent and redefine the use of dance in the "book musical," persevering under the constant pressures of time and money as they embrace the unique qualities that a body moving in space, free from the concrete expressiveness of language, can offer an audience.

NOTES

1. Barbara Stratyner, *Ned Wayburn and the Dance Routine: From Vaudeville to the Ziegfeld Follies* (Studies in Dance History No. 13, Madison: University of Wisconsin Press for the Society of Dance Scholars, 1996).
2. Ned Wayburn, *The Art of Stage Dancing: The Story of a Beautiful and Profitable Profession* (New York: Belvedere, 1980), p. 6.
3. Frank W. D. Ries, "Albertina Rasch: The Broadway Career" (*Dance Chronicle* 6:2 [1983]: 95–137), pp. 95, 99, 101.
4. See Brenda Dixon Gottschild, *Digging the African American Presence in American Performance* (Westport, CT: Praeger, 1996).
5. Jacqui Malone, *Steppin' on the Blues: The Visual Rhythms of African American Dance* (Urbana: University of Illinois Press, 1996), p. 73.
6. Marshall Stearns and Jean Stearns, *Jazz Dance* (New York: Macmillan, 1968), p. 139.
7. John Murray Anderson, *Out without My Rubbers* (New York: Library Publishers, 1954), p. 77.
8. Agnes de Mille, *Martha* (New York: Random House, 1991), p. 68.
9. Richard Kislan, *Hoofing on Broadway: A History of Show Dancing* (New York: Prentice Hall, 1986), p. 57.
10. [a] Frank W. D. Ries, "Sammy Lee: The Broadway Career" (*Dance Chronicle* 9:1 [1986]: 1–95), p. 66.
11. Camille Hardy, Popular Balanchine Dossiers 1927–2004. "*Boys from Syracuse*" (Box 15, New York Public Library for the Performing Arts, Dance Division, New York, NY), p. 13.

12. Constance Valis Hill, Popular Balanchine Dossiers 1927–2004. *"Babes in Arms"* (Box 14, New York Public Library for the Performing Arts, Dance Division, New York, NY), 2002.

13. Barbara Barker, unprocessed papers, box 18, box 5, box 6 (Research materials of Agnes de Mille, New York Public Library for the Performing Arts, Dance Division, New York, NY).

14. Louis Horst, *Modern Dance Forms and Its Relation to the Other Modern Arts* (New York: Dance Horizons, 1961), p. 98.

15. Deborah Jowitt, *Jerome Robbins: His Life, His Theater, His Dance* (New York: Simon & Schuster, 2004), p. 16.

16. Amanda Vaill, *Somewhere: The Life of Jerome Robbins* (New York: Broadway Books, 2006), p. 43.

17. Harriet Johnson, "The First Steps in a Robbins Dance: It's Planning Says *Billion Dollar Baby* Choreographer" (*New York Post*, January 4, 1946).

18. Arthur Gelb, "Robbins and His 'Courage'" (*New York Times* [April 28, 1963]: 127).

19. Judith Brin Ingber, "Dancing into Marriage," *Arabesque* 7.4 (1982): 8–9, 20–21.

20. Greg Lawrence, *Dance with Demons: The Life of Jerome Robbins* (New York: Berkley Books, 2001), p. 342.

21. Jerome Robbins used 1940s and '50s jazz dance from his earliest ballets *Fancy Free* (1944) and *Interplay* (1945 [New York City Ballet premiere 1952]). My focus is on how his interest in combining ballet and jazz found its way to the Broadway stage and to ponder why he did not continue to explore that idiom in the commercial theater after *West Side Story*.

22. Constance Valis Hill, "From Bharata Natyam to Bop: Jack Cole's 'Modern' Jazz Dance" (*Dance Research Journal* 33.2 [Winter 2001–2]: 29–39).

23. Glenn Loney, *Unsung Genius: The Passion of Dancer-Choreographer Jack Cole* (New York: Franklin Watts, 1984), p. 242.

24. Ethel Martin, interview by Liza Gennaro, February 26, 2003, transcript (Oral History Collection, Lincoln Center Library of the Performing Arts, New York, NY).

25. George Beiswanger, "New Images in Dance: Martha Graham and Agnes de Mille" (*Theatre Arts* 28.10 [October 1944]: 609–14), p. 614.

26. Kate Van Winkle Keller and Charles Cyril Hendrickson, *George Washington: A Biography in Social Dance* (Sandy Hook, CT: Hendrickson Group, 1998), p. 109.

27. Genevieve Shimer and Kate van Winkle, *The Playford Ball: 103 Early Country Dances* (Chicago: A Cappella Books and the Country Dance and Song Society, 1990), p. viii.

28. Harvey Evans, interview by Liza Gennaro, March 3, 2003, transcript (Oral History Collection, Lincoln Center Library of the Performing Arts, New York, NY; ◑ Example 4.17).

29. John Anthony Gilvey, *Before the Parade Passes By: Gower Champion and the Glorious American Musical* (New York: St. Martin's Press, 2005), p. 7.

30. Bill T. Jones, telephone interview with Liza Gennaro, May 18, 2007.

PART TWO

TRANSFORMATIONS

5

Minstrelsy and Theatrical Miscegenation

THOMAS L. RIIS

■ □ ■

THE WORD "MINSTREL" DERIVES FROM the Latin term *ministerialis*, an official of the Roman imperial household. From about the twelfth century, the English word denoted a professional entertainer of any kind, but chiefly one who danced, juggled, and played instruments. Up to the late sixteenth century, minstrels were frequently attached to royal courts. Since that time the term has come to suggest a wandering singer or lyric poet equipped with lute, harp, or other portable stringed instrument, since romanticized as a light-hearted rover traversing a pseudo-Medieval landscape. Minstrelsy evokes for modern readers the allure of an idyllic past, often masking the hardscrabble existence of traveling performers.

American minstrelsy—synonymous with blackface minstrelsy because its participants used black face paint (typically a mixture of grease or water and burnt cork from bottle plugs)— arose in the early nineteenth century as a form of mass entertainment. Performers who adopted the name "minstrel" seem to have viewed it as the best moniker at hand to suggest talented artists who upheld professional standards or, ironically, used subversive, carnivalesque elements, or both. The idea to present a *group* of "Ethiopian delineators" (another euphemism for blackface acts) arose from the efforts of innovative circus entertainers to distinguish themselves from competitors.

In June 1842, three white men, Edwin P. Christy, George Harrington, and T. Vaughan, calling themselves the Virginia Minstrels, gave their premiere performance in Buffalo, New York (Harrington's hometown). Christy later attached his own name to the troupe, which enjoyed a long-running success in New York City. The more famous ensemble to use the same name included banjoist Billy Whitlock, songwriter Dan Emmett, and dancers Dick Pelham and Frank Brower, staging a celebrated opening at the Bowery Amphitheater in February 1843. As Dan Emmett later reported the story, they had observed the success of a European singing troupe in America, the Rainers, billed as "the Tyrolese Minstrel Family," and so added the name to a famous Southern state to form the Virginia Minstrels. Both Christy's and Emmett's groups spawned a legion of imitators and within a remarkably short time minstrel fever seized the nation. Formal minstrel companies sprang up, worked steadily across the country, and traveled abroad. Crowds flocked to theaters to see minstrel shows throughout the rest of the nineteenth century.

American minstrelsy was the most influential and long-lived musical-theatrical development in the antebellum period with lingering effects that can be traced to the present. No form of popular entertainment created in the United States since the early nineteenth century has been untouched by it. Thousands of books, songsters, scripts, and music sheets catering to both professional and amateur minstrels were published well into the 1930s. Grounded in what W. T. Lhamon, Jr., has described as "the blackface lore cycle," minstrelsy's basic gestures, expressive patterns, musical incipits, dance steps, and labile attitudes coalesced during the 1820s and 1830s, were transformed and tamed in the 1840s and 1850s, and were further stretched and exploited through the remainder of the century. Although banned or suppressed for its virulent racial stereotyping during the second half of the twentieth century, elements of black-face minstrelsy have repeatedly resurfaced in environments where underclass theatrical expression could come out and be expressed safely—though often indirectly or covertly—in the same venues that fostered rag-time, jazz, rock-and-roll, and hip-hop. Minstrelsy has been and remains a slippery, paradoxical, and tenacious phenomenon.[1]

MISCEGENATION

Because American minstrelsy arose when slavery and the future of social relations among blacks and whites in the United States was being strongly contested, this particular form of blackface theater, more so than any previous one, was preoccupied with the idea of "miscegenation," defined as interracial marriage with the intention of producing mixed-race children. The word was coined in 1863 by Democratic Party propagandist David Goodman Croly, whose anonymously published pamphlet, *Miscegenation: The Theory of the Blending of the Races, Applied to the American White Man and Negro*, alleged that widespread marriage between whites and blacks was the overriding goal of Abraham Lincoln and the Republican Party, as the ultimate solution to interracial conflicts. Although this screed, released during the 1864 presidential campaign to stoke panic among whites, was discredited by the end of the election season, the word nevertheless worked its way into common circulation.

Its Latinate flavor (*miscere*, to mix, plus *genus*, a biological type) lent an air of scientific credibility to the hoax, but "race" as a fixed category was widely accepted as a "natural" and unchangeable human state. To advocate interracial marriage seemed to its detractors to be tantamount to playing God. The scientific basis for racial types is groundless, rooted on surface appearances rather than fundamental genetic differences; all human beings are now classified as *Homo sapiens* and share over 99 percent of their DNA. But the idea was persuasive nonetheless. A rigid set of racial classifications confirmed master-subaltern power relations already established during the slavery period. The common perception of race as an empirical category has determined much American law and custom ever since. Between 1913 and 1948, a majority of American states forbade interracial marriage, although no federal statute was ever enacted to this effect. Only in 1967 did the United States Supreme Court rule all anti-miscegenation laws unconstitutional.

In such a fraught environment, theatrical representation of racial elements and mixing of races on stage (a kind of theatrical miscegenation, which was also illegal in many states), whatever the motive or audience, was bound to be provocative. Every generation of Americans has produced a slightly different reading. Constance Rourke in a famous analysis of American national character detected three archetypal American comic figures: the Yankee peddler, the braggart frontiersman, and the black minstrel.[2] The first two have long since faded from the cultural landscape (or merged with newer types), but the last—being such a mischievous, potent and multivalent figure—is still with us in unsuspected locations.

BLACKFACE BEFORE 1843

The minstrel show, which by 1844 began adhering to consistent formats and advertising itself as a full night's entertainment, comprised a variety of interwoven elements: jokes, dances, patter, topical skits, eccentric instruments, sentimental and comic songs, mimicry of familiar and prominent persons, and much more. With white actor-musicians allegedly imitating the habits and attitudes of African Americans, blackface minstrelsy has been viewed most often as a racist travesty pure and simple. But the roots and the history of minstrelsy are both problematic and complex, and remain the subject of heated debate.[3]

King Richard II reportedly hosted an English royal entertainment that featured characters made up to resemble African potentates in 1377, and Ben Jonson's *Masque of Blackness* (1605) offered a similar conceit, but the most famous of all African or Moorish characters played in blackface by English-speaking actors was Shakespeare's *Othello* (1603), "a general in the service of Venice." This heroic but flawed Moor, created roughly a century after the expulsion of the Moslems from Spain, spawned a variety of serious and comic successors, including musical versions of Aphra Behn's story, *Oroonoko* (1688); George Colman and Samuel Arnold's *Inkle and Yarico* (1787); the comic servant, Mungo, in Bickerstaffe and Dibdin's ballad opera *The Padlock* (1768); and Monostatos in Mozart and Schikaneder's *The Magic Flute* (1791). None of the actors in these plays participated in minstrel troupes as they emerged later, but their conventional black makeup, a mask that enabled the representation of exotic customs or peculiar behavior, laid the foundation for public acceptance of minstrelsy later on. Narratives written by or about escaped slaves further sustained public fascination with African lore and eyewitness travel accounts. But minstrelsy did not take off as a distinctively American phenomenon until the charismatic day-to-day behavior of ordinary African American citizens added another— perhaps the most important—reminder of its immediacy and appeal to the working class.

Folk theatricals or seasonal holiday celebrations with ancient roots also employed blackface performance in unscripted but widely practiced rituals of chaos, such as *Mardi Gras* or Carnival, where all is topsy-turvy. In such celebrations of "misrule," rich and poor, white and black, weak and powerful change costumes and change places—at least for a day—in jovial but sometimes disruptive and even debauched circumstances. Like modern Hallowe'en trick-or-treaters or the saucy exaggerated characters of Italian commedia dell'arte, blackface players in rustic festivals were disguised for fun and profit, but also for protest against social norms. In such a context, blackness was primarily a disguise for safety's sake rather than a racial statement per se.

The creation of the United States in 1789 based on principles of equality for its citizens, New York's Gradual Manumission Law of 1799 (which freed all Negroes born in New York after July 4, 1799), the abolition of slave trade in the British Empire in 1807, and trade patterns established between the United States, England, and the Caribbean islands continued to place the social/political status of dark-skinned and marginalized immigrant peoples at the center of public consciousness. The construction of the Erie Canal (1817–25), which required mass employment of unskilled labor, brought darker working-class newcomers inland, affecting northern and western regions of the country as well as the South. Canals historian Peter Way reports that the work was "performed by the lowest of the low, Irish immigrants and slaves. [Done by] these two pariah groups, ... canalling [became] one of the first truly lumpen proletarian professions in North America."[4] Yet these workers, along with other riverboat men, itinerant tradespeople, trappers, and explorers were heroic in their way and lived on as romantic figures in later nostalgic song. Songs and plays of the time manifested both sympathy for the enslaved or newly freed workers, and fearful suspicion about their place in the social order.

Andrew Jackson's election in 1828—closely following complete emancipation in the state of New York in 1827—marked another sea change, as America's elite old guard was visibly contesting with a restless underclass and working class hoping for advancement. The movement of the American national boundary to the west, and the accompanying influx of Easterners, new European immigrants, and former slaves— ever more deeply encroaching into Native American territory— and the disappearance of massive agriculturally based slavery above the Mason-Dixon line fed sectional debates about slavery, miscegenation, and the significance of racial difference across the country. Huge population increases during the first decades of the nineteenth century complicated life in the cities, forcing the issues of urban subsistence, family formation, patriotism, and personal identity. Minstrels of the 1830s sang about the yearnings of all racial groups. Some took up the cause of Andrew Jackson, especially his opposition to the rechartering of a national bank, and of struggling northern black workers, by means of the foppish figure known as Zip Coon. Apart from and yet related to English scripted stage traditions were folk-inspired improvisational ones. Minstrel shows drew from both streams, featuring soloists, duets, trios, and larger ensembles performing on noisy, eccentric instruments, dancing wildly in tattered costumes, and singing raucous comic songs such as "Buffalo Gals" (referring to the city, not bison), which probably dates to 1844:

> Buffalo gals, won't you come out tonight,
> Come out tonight, come out tonight.
> Buffalo gals, won't you come out tonight
> And dance by the light of the moon.

Well before the advent of the mass-marketed minstrel show, American improvisational actors were busy imitating African Americans—not only exotic Africans—in broad and memorable gestures. They claimed to have encountered their models for impersonation on southern plantations, western riverboats, and in northern urban neighborhoods. The roots of many minstrel controversies lie in the credibility of these claims. One of the earliest paradoxes of minstrel research is that minstrel shows, while claiming southern Negro roots—seem to have first appeared and had their greatest impact in northeastern cities performed by white men during the 1840s. Minstrel-like ensembles developed in many locations, but minstrelsy became a mass cultural phenomenon with the help of modern technology, transportation, and communication networks provided by cities, especially port cities such as Buffalo, Albany, Philadelphia, and New York.

The neighborhood of Five Points, near Catherine Market, a formerly bustling commercial crossroads on the East River between Brooklyn and south Manhattan, was an especially fecund spot for pre-minstrel doings. A place where racial groups intermingled in the late eighteenth and early nineteenth centuries, this area thrust together its inhabitants and facilitated cross-cultural contact and exchange. Participating in the bustling life on the wharves and markets of New York's Seventh Ward, black men contested with each other and were paid in money or in goods to entertain and drum up business for shopkeepers. Black step-dancers went about this activity and were sketched by a local witness as early as 1820. By 1848, their demonstrations—"dancing for eels" as it was termed at the time—were taken up as theatrical skits in plays by Frank Chanfrau in the nearby Chatham Theatre and were preserved in genre paintings by William Sidney Mount (1807–68).

Outside observers of Five Points during the 1850s raised objections to what was plainly normal everyday behavior for the residents—not only the mixing of people of different races in public markets and social spaces, but the free and easy attitudes of the local women in their exchanges with men, at a level of frivolity that disrupted the habits favored by merchants who depended on a large group of docile factory workers from this same laboring class. Class critics noticed and scoffed at the deliberate use of theatrical devices—peculiar dress, accents, perfume, and makeup in places of amusement or public gatherings—which further muddy the waters of identity and imitation. As is clear from many accounts, poor white residents of Catherine Market were not dressing down simply to mock their dark-skinned neighbors but rather to flatter them or pay compliments by trading songs, jibes, jokes, and stories in a free-flowing exchange that touched observers within and without, high, low or middle in status.

While outsiders may have viewed the whole spectacle of rough fun as devoid of middle-class decorum, evidence for minstrel vitality is everywhere apparent, in their lyrics, repetitive choruses that invite participation, the illustrations provided in songsters, and the newspapers and police records when ebullient spirits erupted violently or spilled over disruptively into more genteel venues.

> I come to town de udder night.
> I hear da noise, den saw de fight.
> De watchman was a runnin' roun'.
> Cryin' Old Dan Tucker's come to town.
> So get out de way! Get out de way!
> Get out de way! Old Dan Tucker
> You're too late to come to supper.

T.D. RICE

Thomas Dartmouth ("Daddy") Rice (1808–60), a resident of the Bowery and frequent denizen of Five Points and Catherine Market, was centrally important to the rise and spread of blackface entertainment. Born into a poor Anglo-American Protestant family, Rice trained as a ship carver's apprentice but also acted in modestly appointed local theaters—often these were little more than saloons with raised platforms for the performers—which offered farces, melodramas, and topical skits. He would soon be playing to vast crowds in New York and London, having perfected his unusual talent on the road.

Rice's lasting impact was made with the songs and acts he developed as a traveling showman beginning in 1828. The most sensational was "Jim Crow," a dancing song in which he mimicked country or street characters. The faithfulness of his imitations were attested by those professionals closest to him, but the power of his unique impersonations seems to have come from an intense combination of elements: motley clothes, a blackened face, a twisted and turning body (knees bent, left hand raised, and right arm akimbo); and transgressive ideas sung and spoken in the manner of an ancient court jester, albeit in rough quasi-black dialect. He often spoke for and not against the black race and found a sympathetic audience among the white working class as well. Jim Crow in Rice's depiction was a proud, free, defiant, and slippery trickster, impossible to account for and never accountable to authority figures or powerful institutions.

> Weel about and turn about and do jis so;
> Eb'ry time I weel about, I jump Jim Crow

Speaking on behalf of the marginalized and against the rich and prominent, Rice's fame spread dramatically throughout America and England during the 1830s. He almost always played to audiences mixed by race and class. As one of his managers, Frank Wemyss, reported in 1848, "Mr. Rice crossed the Atlantic [during 1837], and turned the heads of the chimney sweeps and apprentice boys of London, who wheeled about and turned about and jumped Jim Crow, from morning until night, to the annoyance of their masters, but the great delight of the cockneys." It was Rice's peculiar brand of acting that helped to reveal the vast potential for developing more extended full-evening shows, minstrelsy that encompassed plays with interpolated songs, vocal ensembles, group dances, and circus specialties.

As Dale Cockrell has extensively documented, blackface theater was not restricted to or developed solely on the minstrel stage.[5] Rice was only one of several white actors engaged in blackface antics. Others included theater manager/comedian Englishman Charles Mathews who in 1822 claimed to be satirizing a black American actor (probably James Hewitt) in his London acts, and white American George Washington Dixon (1801–61) whose vehicles included dialect songs such as "Coal Black Rose" and "Zip Coon" (also known as "Turkey in the Straw"). Gradually in the 1830s, other singing actors began to add dancers and instrumentalists to their acts with African instruments or instruments associated with southern slaves, such as bone castanets, fiddles, tambourines, banjos, and sometimes accordions or concertinas. Solo turns became ensemble acts with four or more members. For individual singers, the term "minstrel" could still be loosely applied until 1843, but the arrival of Dan Emmett's quartet in New York established a prototype for the term and its synonyms, "harmonist" and "serenader."

FROM 1843 TO THE CIVIL WAR AND BEYOND

In the antebellum era, blackface minstrelsy dominated the American popular theater to the exclusion of all other forms. A variety of formats were introduced, but all included a few essential ingredients. A small group of men in blackface played noisy instruments, sang lively dialect songs—often parodies—and performed satirical skits. Most shows concluded with a vigorous dance finale. Many troupes took to the road and many others established themselves full-time in locations and theater buildings reserved for minstrelsy exclusively. Within a year of the Virginia Minstrels' New York debut, another minstrel troupe, the Ethiopian Serenaders, was appearing in the White House (see Figure 5.1). By 1846 this ambitious ensemble set out to perform in England and was well received. Minstrel troupes blanketed towns along the Ohio and Mississippi rivers, set up shop in all large cities, and traveled to California with the Gold Rush of 1849. The most prominent companies before 1850 included the Virginia Minstrels, Christy Minstrels, Ethiopian Serenaders, Buckley's Congo Minstrels, and the New Orleans Serenaders. Ordway's Aeolians, Wood's Minstrels, White's Serenaders, and Sanford's Opera Troupe, among many others, flourished through the 1850s.[6]

By the late 1840s, as minstrel show production methods became more settled and established, managers sought to widen their audience and soften the edginess of their repertory. The irreverence of the early days was mitigated, though not replaced, by aspirations for respectability and a larger number of paying customers, including women and children. The descriptions of comfortable theater interiors of the time also imply that a more genteel audience was being sought. Emphasis continued to be placed on dialect songs and burlesques—the latter often focusing on English and Italian operas (for example, Balfe's *The Bohemian Girl* or Bellini's *Norma*)—but more instrumental solos and sentimental parlor songs were interpolated as well. Theater seating capacity was expanded and liquor was banned. The intensely parodic quality of minstrel humor was maintained. No prominent persons, political figures, foreign groups, or exotic ideas were exempt from ridicule. All current events and upper-class fashions became objects of fun. Stump

FIGURE 5.1 Sheet music cover: "Music of the Ethiopian Serenaders." (Reproduction courtesy of the American Music Research Center, University of Colorado, Boulder)

speeches and tall tales were the order of the day, the wilder the better.

Roles were designated for the instrumentalists on the front line. The tambourine player (Mr. Tambo) and the bone castanet player (Mr. Bones) stood on either end of a semicircle of anywhere from four to eight men and joked with each other as a prelude to a series of musical or other specialties. To underline the increasing impulse to control eccentric minstrel movements and manners among polite audiences, a third character, Mr. Interlocuter, who always spoke with perfect diction and unctuous tone, arose in the 1850s to stand center stage and serve as master of ceremonies. His traditional opening line underscores his task to rein in potentially disruptive forces: "Gentlemen, be seated!" In the 1850s and 1860s, pro-black sentiments were less in evidence than they had been in T. D. Rice's shows, and blackface performers became blank slates inscribable with any sort of comic twist.

Minstrel humor, while certainly racist after 1843, was not invariably so, although stereotypical markers of blackness were consistently employed. Minstrelsy held up to ridicule foreign performers such as violinist Ole Bull or singer Jenny Lind, but it also exposed pompous preachers and greedy capitalists, and spoke to various issues with no direct tie to African American culture. If, for example, the idea of phrenology—reading bumps on the head to gauge character and personality—were a fashionable topic, then minstrels would deliver absurd dialect speeches on the subject. When the flashy French conductor Louis Jullien (1812–60) brought his eighty-seven-piece orchestra to New York in 1853, the same season as opera diva Anne Seguin appeared, with both charging the public large fees to attend their concerts, they were roundly put down by Buckley's Serenaders' skits about "the Black Jew-Lion" and "Mme. Anna See-Her." Since tickets to the Serenaders show were only twelve-and-a-half cents, the class-based critique of elevated European tastes and exhibitions was especially pointed.

Because of its commanding place in mid-century American culture, minstrelsy—not unlike television in a later era—had occasion to weigh in on every conceivable subject from temperance to women's rights. Minstrel scripts and period playbills address an array of topics related to gender, class, politics, and musical taste, as well as race. Typical minstrel show "finales" found in advertisements in the 1840s and 1850s allude to other theater pieces as well as fads and current events, and include, for example, "Fireman's Chaunt," "Burlesque Tragedy of Damon and Pythias," and "Burlesque of the Bohemian Girl."

Blackface minstrelsy grew and changed with a protean character that defies full explanation. It did far more than borrow surface racial features or allow itself to be limited to a single signifier. Minstrelsy rarely if ever attempted to say much about Africa or "the old plantation" as a real place, but it often provided a disguise or mask behind which actors could comment on the American scene—urban, suburban, rural—in the form of a burlesque. Any claims that minstrelsy portrayed "authentic" African American culture must be weighed against its essentially satirical character. Minstrels were never trying to score serious aesthetic points or make idealistic declarations. Rather, they subjected all types of foreignness, pretension, or posturing to close scrutiny and broad lampoon. How to explain the strong presence of operatic parody embedded in 1840s and 1850s minstrelsy but from a need to critique the strong presence of European visitors on American stages?

Such was the power and flexibility of the minstrel format and its reputation for rambunctious irreverence that African Americans themselves began to form minstrel companies in the 1850s, although most of the early troupes were short-lived. Immediately following the Civil War, however, minstrelsy became one of the most important points of entry for young, ambitious Negro men seeking a nonfarm livelihood and a ticket to the big city. Brooker and Clayton's Georgia Minstrels emerged in 1865, closely followed by a series of companies created by Lew Johnson and Charles B. Hicks. These African American impresarios traveled the world—from South America and Australia to Asia and of course Europe—in treks that sustained the fame of "genuine" black minstrels for decades. Ike Simond in his autobiographical "reminiscence and pocket history of the colored profession," published in 1891, names hundreds of minstrels unrecorded in any other source.[7] The history of African American minstrelsy in the late nineteenth century is still largely untold.

GENDER AND MINSTRELSY

Misogyny was an especial preoccupation of mid-nineteenth-century minstrel shows. Offered primarily to male audiences by male actors, minstrel shows consistently instructed men on the wiles, charms, moods, ruses, and demands of women in and out of marriage and the home. Many men specialized in cross-dressing parts to establish the illusion of a feminine presence or to set up scenes of romance gone awry. George Harrington, one of E. P. Christy's first partners, was famed for his "wench" roles, as was Tony Hart (1855–91), partner of Ned Harrigan.

Few real women worked in minstrelsy, but opportunities for men to do cross-gender burlesque were plentiful. As early as 1847, an ensemble calling itself "Female American Serenaders," probably only female in costume, performed a noisy minstrel finale entitled "Railroad Overture." Minstrel men regularly imitated the attitudes and dances of famous women performers, such as Jenny Lind and Fanny Elssler. The minstrel show remained men's business, and cross-dressing actors were common in the 1840s and later. Francis Leon, the most prominent of female impersonators, who trained as a minstrel before the war, was billed as "the Only Leon," and had perfected the role of prima donna by 1870. By giving complete attention to every facet of his elaborate wardrobe (including dozens of custom-made dresses and expensive jewelry), makeup, and movement, he portrayed a subtle and serious image of ideal femininity, not a farcical take-off.

THE MUSIC OF THE MINSTREL SHOW

One of the bedeviling aspects of minstrel show history, partly accounting for its hold on successive generations despite repulsive racist and sexist elements, is its large and attractive musical repertory. By the mid-1840s, minstrelsy had come to be understood by many as a basic framework, hospitable to the latest musical novelty. Much of the music was composed by performers in shows who needed to dance, sing, and play at the same time, and the numbers were stitched together from a mixture of elements. Audience preference for a busy stage presence encouraged a less complex musical structure within individual numbers than would have been required for, say, a solo concert recitalist.

Such popular favorites as "Old Dan Tucker" had many verses with a relatively short and repetitive melody (Example 5.1). The song could accommodate a nearly endless series of tempos, poses, asides, and elaborations. Minstrel songs not only allowed but required a sustained intensity in performance in order to make the most of their basic material. Only the performers who could ratchet up a song's energy succeeded on a large scale. This combination of simple musical building blocks and broad physical gestures defined the quintessentially American quality of minstrelsy. More than mere musical medleys interspersed with comic dialogues, minstrel shows presented a crescendo of intensity realized through a concatenation of events. It riveted audiences with a rich interactive rhetoric of gesture and movement, lively tunes, and humorous speech.

Many minstrel songs from the early years have survived in memory into the twenty-first century, having become a permanent part of America's collective consciousness. Stephen Foster (1826–64) was arguably the finest native-born songwriter of the minstrel era. His melodies were reprinted in European sources as early as the 1850s. He wrote specifically for the Christy Minstrels, although many other groups adopted his most popular numbers, including "Gentle Annie," "Oh Susanna," "Camptown Races," "Old Folks at Home," and "Old Uncle Ned." Many of his lyrics capture the manic absurdity of the minstrel persona as well as its sentimental turns.

> It rained so hard the day I left,
> The weather it was dry.
> The sun so hot, I froze to death.
> Susannah, don't you cry.

Minstrel songs enabled expressions of pathos, satire, and energetic good fun, within singable melodies with regular rhythms, punctuating chords, and accompanying percussion. Much of the raw material was original, but much was also reshaped from preexisting sources: banjo and fiddle tunes from the oral/aural tradition, Irish melodies, current favorites from the opera stage, and parlor songs. As harmonized choral concerts of Negro spirituals became the rage in the 1870s and 1880s, inspired by the success of the Fisk Jubilee Singers, traveling minstrel companies wasted no time in incorporating them into their repertory and making fun of them as well (🞊 Example 5.2).

Rag music was first published during the 1890s, when it became a national craze. The new *style*—first understood as a rhythmically inflected type suitable for exuberant and syncopated dancing (as opposed to a *genre* of music called ragtime)—had unquestioned roots in midwestern African American communities. It differed from minstrelsy, at least for black composers, in its refusal to be identified as imitation or parody of something else. Yet because it was understood as a black genre, whites wrote and sang ragtime songs in blackface, adding words that reinscribed hackneyed racial stereotypes. The specific subgenre of ragtime songs that uses insulting dialect verses is referred to as "coon song."

By the 1890s minstrelsy had ceased to command the attention of crowds in theaters devoted to that purpose. No new music was being composed for the genre. But the explosion in sheet music publication, including colorful cover illustrations—with both drawings and photographs—proved that the visual legacy of minstrel grotesques remained (see Figure 5.2). Distorted faces, wildly gesticulating characters, clothed apes, razor-wielding toughs, chicken-stealing hoodlums, and sultry females ushered in a new era of hard-edged and brutal images, bespeaking anxiety about overcrowded ethnic enclaves in American cities at the turn of the century. Many of the lyrics and covers amount to racial slander. By the 1920s, this type of song lyric had been supplanted by the blues and less virulent verses in Tin Pan Alley products, but the exaggerated images persisted on title pages, posters, songsters, and films.

The 1890s also saw the creation of the first all-black cast and black-created musical comedies, many of which made a point of not using burnt cork even while incorporating "coon" songs and every other kind of ethnic humor imaginable. Robert "Bob" Cole and his partner Billy Johnson in their landmark show, *A Trip to Coontown* (1898), featured a succession of ethnic imitations by popular comedian Tom Brown, including an Italian, a "Chinaman," and an Irish policemen. Cole himself took the role of a lovable hobo who appeared in *white* face makeup—possibly a model for both Charlie Chaplin and circus clown Emmett Kelly.[8] Offering both farce comedy and a parody of the popular contemporary musical *A Trip to Chinatown*, Cole and Johnson's effort lasted only a few seasons on the road

FIGURE 5.2 Sheet music cover: "Oh! Didn't It Rain," featuring Eddie
Leonard. (Reproduction courtesy of the American Music Research Center,
University of Colorado, Boulder)

but proved that black actors and creators could successfully challenge the long-lived stereotypes of minstrelsy, spawning at least two dozen similar shows over the next two decades.

The most successful African American actor at the turn of the century, famous for boldly crossing the color line at the highest level, retained blackface for his entire career. The Ziegfeld Follies star, Bert Williams (1874–1922) could have followed the lead of his friends Bob Cole and Ernest Hogan (the self-proclaimed "unbleached American"), but Williams confessed to never having felt comfortable onstage *without* burnt cork—such was the strength of the convention throughout his early career. Personal accounts of those who saw him, as well as surviving film clips of his most famous skits, give powerful evidence of a superbly skilled actor who managed to transcend the limited realm of contemporary white minstrels with his own personal gestures and style, underlain by a deep strain of melancholy. W. C. Fields famously called Williams, "the funniest man I ever saw, and the saddest man I ever knew."

MINSTRELSY IN FILM

The earliest films about African American life, from the late 1890s, were short newsreels or documentaries capturing brief moments of unscripted action (e.g., a watermelon-eating contest, West Indian boys at play, African American soldiers disembarking from ships returned from the Spanish American War). But "black" characters were acted by whites in blackface so frequently that the appearance of real African Americans onscreen assumed a parallel, but distinctly different, path for blacks than for whites playing black roles.

Because much of early moviemaking was about getting the product to market rapidly and cheaply, filmmakers tended to adopt the most vivid images already in circulation, including stereotyped figures from the minstrel stage: olive-complexioned women with "tragic" (i.e., mixed race) personal histories, predatory young men adrift in the city, and hordes of dancing, singing "darkies" at every street corner. For nostalgia fans—who were many—the movies provided familiar plantation characters and antebellum scenarios featuring full-figured mammies, docile Uncle Toms, and happy hyperactive children. Minstrel images were transferred directly from the stage to films, dominating the portrayals of most real African American characters in the first two decades of the twentieth century even as independent black filmmakers William Foster and Oscar Micheaux made their first movies.

The most important film in the pre–sound era to include black characters, both real and blackface, was D. W. Griffith's *The Birth of a Nation* (1915). It astonished its first viewers by telling a sweeping Reconstruction-era story of the founding of the Ku Klux Klan, heroically reclaiming the South from heartless Yankee carpetbaggers and freedmen run amok. Using virtuoso cinematic techniques studied by film students to this day, *The Birth of a Nation* flagrantly perpetuated degrading stereotypes of hulking, frenzied black males raping, pillaging, and generally wreaking havoc. Black women were either scheming seductresses or repulsive hags. Griffith's wish to convey the devastation of civil war and its aftermath was realized, ironically, to the detriment of some of its most oppressed victims.

The overwhelming success of *The Birth of a Nation* gave new life to the most loathsome minstrel images for at least a generation. White vaudeville headliner Al Jolson in blackface famously sang "Mammy" in *The Jazz Singer* (1927) as he inaugurated the new era of sound films. Director Erich von Stroheim courageously placed African Americans in complex roles within a biracial cast in such films as *Wedding March* (1928), and King Vidor would feature musical African

Americans in *Hallelujah!* in 1929, but not until more subtle technical effects were possible on screen in the 1930s did a few independent Hollywood filmmakers expand their horizons and invite individual actors to discard minstrel-based stereotypes. The work of Nina Mae McKinney, Clarence Muse, Bill "Bojangles" Robinson, Willie Best, Mantan Moreland, Eddie "Rochester" Anderson, Paul Robeson, Louise Beavers, Fredi Washington, and Rex Ingraham was prominent in this period. Herb Jeffries, as "The Bronze Buckeroo," appeared in black-cast Westerns. Black gangster films were made by Apollo Theater entrepreneur Ralph Cooper. Hattie McDaniel, as a classic minstrel mammy—albeit more humanely realized than most—won the Academy Award for Best Supporting Actress for her performance in *Gone With the Wind* (1939). Films of the late 1940s and '50s were still dominated by African American characters whose chief job was to sing, grin, and dance.[9]

After the radical displacements of World War II, besides the enhanced visibility of the real black community in America and the internationally recognized heroism of black troops, more significant changes appeared to be possible. Hollywood gradually showed itself willing to treat racial issues seriously. The Academy Award nomination of Dorothy Dandridge in the title role of *Carmen Jones* (1954) and Sidney Poitier's appearance in the *Edge of the City* (1957) were positive signs of change. Black agency in the television and film industry was enhanced gradually with the increase in number of African American actors of the first rank and the emergence of young independent black filmmakers, most prominently Melvin Van Peeples (*Sweet Sweetback's Baaadasssss Song*, 1971) and Spike Lee (*Do the Right Thing*, 1989; *Jungle Fever*, 1991; and *Bamboozled*, 2000—the last film imagines a successful recreation of a blackface minstrel show on modern television).

CONCLUSION

Although the diversity of visual representations of race has increased in complexity across the United States and around the world during the last third of the twentieth century and into the twenty-first, and while many old-fashioned minstrel stereotypes have lost their ability to shock (or even surprise) us, the association of black-face makeup with motives of racial mockery and denigration is by no means dead. In 2004, gay white comedian Chuck Knipp created an outrageous black female stage character named Shirley Q. Liquor and drew howls of protest from feminists and antiracists who happened to notice the show in a downtown New York nightclub. (Incidentally, Knipp also found enthusiastic support from the black drag queen Ru Paul.) Clearly minstrelsy as a site for parody, comedy, and burlesque in the classic sense is still very much with us. Blackface remains a lightning rod for expressions of opinion about larger sociopolitical questions. The sprightly musical residue of early minstrelsy has largely been separated out from its racialized images and texts (now habitually bowdlerized), so as to facilitate the incorporation of the tunes into generic folk song histories appropriate for children.

NOTES

1. For further readings, see Thomas Riis, American Minstrel Music (Oxford Bibliographies Online, 2016).
2. Constance Rourke, *American Humor: A Study of the National Character* (Garden City, NY: Doubleday, 1953; originally published 1931).
3. On this subject, see especially Eric Lott, *Love and Theft: Blackface Minstrelsy and the American Working Class* (New York: Oxford University Press, 1993).

4. W. T. Lhamon, Jr., *Raising Cain: Blackface Performance from Jim Crow to Hip Hop* (Cambridge, MA: Harvard University Press, 1998), p. 62.
5. Dale Cockrell, *Demons of Disorder: Early Blackface Minstrels and Their World* (Cambridge: Cambridge University Press, 1997).
6. William J. Mahar, *Behind the Burnt Cork Mask: Early Blackface Minstrelsy and Antebellum American Popular Culture* (Urbana: University of Illinois Press, 1999), pp. 355–63.
7. Ike Simond, *Old Slack's Reminiscence and Pocket History of the Colored Profession from 1865 to 1891* (Reprint edition, Popular Press: Bowling Green, OH, 1974; originally published 1891), pp. xvii–xxiii.
8. This suggestion comes to me from David Krasner, author of *Resistance, Parody and Double Consciousness in African American Theatre, 1895–1910* (New York: St. Martin's Press, 1997), and Marvin McAllister, author of *White People Do Not Know How to Behave at Entertainments Designed for Ladies and Gentlemen of Colour* (Chapel Hill: University of North Carolina Press, 2003).
9. See Donald Bogle, *Toms, Coons, Mulattoes, Mammies, and Bucks: An Interpretive History of Blacks in American Films,* 4th ed. (New York: Continuum, 2001).

6

Tin Pan Alley Songs
on Stage and Screen
Before World War II

RAYMOND KNAPP AND MITCHELL MORRIS

■ □ ■

TIN PAN ALLEY HAS SUFFERED from a bad reputation, and the company it has kept has not helped it any: Broadway, Hollywood, and the American musical on the one hand, and jazz (back when it was disreputable), radio crooning, and popular singers and groups on the other. Indeed, jazz's practitioners, fans, and historians, in elevating jazz to its latter-day position of "America's classical music," have tended to overlook or downplay its awkward dependence on Tin Pan Alley, which provided many of the tunes that brought jazz its mainstream popularity. But whereas jazz historians might easily claim, if disingenuously, that Tin Pan Alley's tunes provided only a starting point for a jazz number, and only in some cases, those tunes in their original versions were most often the core attraction in the Broadway and Hollywood musicals that figure most prominently in historical surveys. As a result, historians of the musical have had to perform their own quaint dance around Tin Pan Alley, focusing mostly on revivable shows and films with enduring repute, and placing their focus on what the songs in such shows accomplish, usually through being "integrated" (see chapters 3 and 7). Like jazz historians, they rarely bother to note how often those songs also serve—deliberately and even proudly—a broader marketplace.

In this chapter, we consider the extensive overlap, before World War II, of Tin Pan Alley with Broadway, vaudeville, and post-1927 Hollywood, a convergence that includes not only the well-known shows and films from this period, but also those shows and films that are most frequently overlooked by historians: revues, variety shows, and musical comedies whose musical numbers were only loosely held together by a plot or theme. On Broadway, such shows included not only Ziegfeld's Follies and similar "annual" fare[1] but also book shows that counted on hit tunes for their sustainability—in other words, almost everything except operetta, and even some of that repertory. In Hollywood, there were first of all the correlatives of staged revues, such as Busby Berkeley's "Gold Digger" films (1933–1937), the "Big Broadcast" and "Broadway Melody" films (1936–1940), and *The Goldwyn Follies* (1938). But there was also the rampant practice, within the Hollywood studio system, of song substitution in adaptations of stage shows, which, before cast albums stabilized the song lists of stage shows (beginning in the 1940s), most often resulted in fewer than half of a film's songs coming from the show it ostensibly adapted for the screen. These films all fall irretrievably on the disdained side of the dichotomy evoked by John L. Sullivan, the would-be idealistic film director of Preston Sturges's *Sullivan's Travels* (1941) who is eager to move on from *Ants in Your Plants of 1939* to the social realism of *O Brother, Where Art Thou*. For better or worse, Sullivan's dichotomy is one we seem to be stuck with, despite the realization that comes to Sullivan himself in his "travels": "There's a lot to be said for making people laugh. Did you know that that's all some people have? It isn't much, but it's better than nothing in this cock-eyed caravan."

These shows and films don't (for the most part) have a privileged place in histories of the American musical, nor can their neglected history be captured in an essay of this scope. Fortunately, the basic events of this era may be easily researched in Gerald Bordman's compendious *American Musical Theatre* and/or the Internet Broadway Database.[2] More consistent with the aims of this collection, and with our desire to throw emphasis toward the songs themselves, is for us to place this extensive oeuvre within those histories that are better known, by briefly describing the forces that shaped venues for popular song during the Tin Pan Alley era, establishing the cultural function of the songs thus produced, and explaining how the quintessential type of Tin Pan Alley song developed so as to serve not only shows and films but also other markets, including sheet music, recordings, radio, and jazz-based venues and markets. To this end, we will probe the cultural work done by some of the highly problematic songs of this era, sketch the historical basis for the intertwined histories of Broadway and Tin Pan Alley both before and after the "Great War," query the codification of the mature Tin Pan Alley type between the wars, and discuss—following Rose Rosengard Subotnik's brave lead—the ways in which the songs of this era, largely *because* of their quotidian nature, have continued to provide essential "Equipment for Living."[3]

EARLY TIN PAN ALLEY AND THE SOCIAL FABRIC

A quick survey of any large list of songs performed in musical plays and revues on the New York stage at the turn of the century reveals a bemusing concentration of numbers that project clusters of racial and ethnic stereotypes. "Coon songs," in particular, owe the majority of their musical and lyrical styles as well as their customary performance practices to minstrelsy, but over and above their ways of imagining the appearance and habits of African Americans, they also decisively shape the ways that other minorities appear in the popular music of the time. The lavish array of social (stereo)types was perhaps especially important because of the mileu in which they were generated. New York City's overwhelming importance as a destination for immigrants, along with the population density created especially by the city's tenement system,[4] guaranteed that citizens would frequently cross paths with a wide assortment of people who could be sorted into racial or ethnic "groups."[5] (The modes of social identification/recognition cut across class and economic lines as well, but by and large immigrants tended to start out very poor.) In an oft-cited remark, progressive journalist Jacob Riis in his 1890 book *How the Other Half Lives* asserted that a map of New York coded by ethnicity "would show more stripes than on the skin of the zebra and more colors than the rainbow."[6] And, regrettably but not surprisingly, interactions among the ethnic groups settled in the city could become vicious. The most famous instance of this was the New York City Draft Riot of 1863, in which immigrant resentment against the draft—especially sharp because well-off draftees could pay their way out of enlistment and impoverished newcomers had no such option—led to numerous atrocities against the scapegoated African American population of the city. But this was only one of a series of episodes of mass violence that sporadically broke out during the nineteenth century (and well into the twentieth century); in between such times of uncontrollable hostility, there was a steady underscore of bad feeling, from distrust to dislike to outright hostility, always present.

In an environment of such persistent tension between groups, the ethnic caricatures that litter the New York stage may well seem to have been an improvement over homicidal rage and malice. That is, even ambivalent laughter (both with the figures and at them) could seem to have the potential to reduce ethnic tensions by substituting travesty for assault and battery. From another point of view, since such stock figures quite often carry attributes that could be treated as backhand compliments, attention to the positive aspects of these cartoons, though still stereotypical, might lead audiences to at least limited forms of tolerance as well. Moreover, it can be argued that one of the greatest challenges of an urban environment of such extreme variety as New York is acquiring the forms of social tact that will allow different groups to manage, if not avoid entirely, potential offenses against one another. To some extent this challenge is a question of "knowing one's place" literally as well as figuratively, but it also entails developing a template of routines—a system of manners—that enable further interactions with familiar groups as well as methods of coping with groups previously unencountered. The problem with such strategies is that their possible effectiveness in the theater may stop at the exit; there are no good reasons to have confidence that what works to defuse animosity onstage will also work offstage. But whether or not these ethnic songs had any beneficial effects in everyday life at the turn of the century, they carry historical importance for scholars of the musical not least because their practical realizations can end up undermining the manifest content of the stereotypes that the songs project.

"How Can They Tell That Oi'm Irish?" was a successful song in the Broadway show *The Jolly Bachelors* from 1910. The show was built on a wafer-thin plot in which three men compete for the affections of an heiress, one Astarita Vandergould (played by the popular vaudeville star Nora Bayes), who has taken a job as a drugstore clerk in order to find a boyfriend. But Bayes was well known (and well liked) for her propensity to step out of character and simply sing popular songs to the audience. It is clear that this is the case here.[7] The song's persona is that of a newly arrived immigrant who is determined to pass as "American," and cannot understand why her masquerade does not work. The first verse sets the scene:

> I landed here from Ireland just a week ago today,
> And as soon as I had settled in the town
> I resolved to act entirely in a Yankee Doodle way,
> So I changed me name but not me emerald gown.

Unfortunately for the song's protagonist, her accent is quite broad—but she seems not to hear that. Bayes puts on a brogue (a brogue that the song's persona denies having) and decorates her performance with the occasional hoydenish yip and yodel. The musical setting is not marked with any Irishisms: no bagpipe figures or jiggish rhythms, nothing to connect it to overgeneralizations of Irish folk music. Rather, the stereotype is situated firmly in the realm of accent and diction—details of speech that it is implied the character is too naive or unintelligent to notice. Instead, she wanders around her new town constantly puzzled that everyone she encounters instantly knows her origins (🜊 Example 6.1).

To be sure, the humor here is not particularly pointed; its derogatory content is more potential than actual. In this, it fits well with the trend of Irish stereotyping at the turn of the century; nastier ethnic caricatures were much more common earlier in the nineteenth century, and by the 1890s Irishness was increasingly an excuse for effusive sentiment rather than ethnic denigration. The song's typing is made considerably less stable, moreover, by the layering of Nora Bayes's own persona. A Jewish girl from Illinois (her birth name was Eleanor Goldberg), Bayes anglicized herself by stage name and by several of her marriages.[8] As mentioned earlier, her character in *The Jolly Bachelors* is named Astarita Vandergould—its very implausibility does not detract from its function as a parody of "Old New York" high society.[9] So what might it have meant for a Jewish comedienne passing as Anglo, playing an "old money" New Yorker disguised as a shop girl, to step out of character and take on an Irish persona? In any case, the possibilities of a kind of ethnic delirium were quite high, and arguably such play with identity added significantly to the song's appeal.

Prejudices against other ethnic groups can be more tenaciously ugly in the comic songs of the period. "Chin Chin Chinaman" was one of the most popular hits from *The Geisha*, a British musical comedy that was first performed in London in 1896 and was hugely successful in New York that same year.[10] A bargain-counter variation of Gilbert and Sullivan's 1885 hit *The Mikado, The Geisha* tells a romantic story of courtship between the handsome British naval officer Reggie Fairfax (already engaged to Molly, a girl back home) and the beautiful young geisha O Mimosa San. Shades of Cio Cio San! But no, the plot of this work does not take the tragic turn found in David Belasco's play *Madame Butterfly* (1900) and Puccini's operatic adaption (1904); instead, in *The Geisha* the kind of switched-identity shenanigans common in farce ensure that the romantic leads end up with partners of the appropriate social and racial position. The character Captain Wun-Hi, the Chinese proprietor of the Japanese Tea House employing Mimosa (against all historical likelihood), is clearly comic relief, and "Chin Chin Chinaman" is his one song.

One of the earliest recorded versions of the song is a rendition by James T. Powers, a New York comedian who found one of his major roles in revival productions of the show.[11] The recording begins with a histrionic fanfare of fake Chinese, after which the song settles into an absolutely regular 4×4 verse-chorus structure. The musical setting is quite minimal, probably to provide room for the performer's comic effects— not only the stream of faux-discourse that starts the number, but also especially the strange parodic cadenza that ends the recording. This is not "real" (i.e., Western) virtuosity, but a clumsy musical imitation. As for the lyrics, they are put into the style by which Chinese-accented English is usually derided (🔊 Example 6.2):

> Chin chin Chinaman/Muchee Muchee sad!
> Me afraid allo trade/Wellee welle bad!
> Noee joke—/Brokee broke—/Makee shuttee shop!
> Chin chin Chinaman/Chop, chop, chop!

The strategy of mockery is obvious in the lyrics' jeering focus on the character's inability to distinguish between "l" and "r" and his addition of extra vowels on many of the words that end in consonants.[12] The inability to pronounce English correctly is the verbal equivalent of his unsuccessful musical aspirations. But it is worth noting as well that in the midst of all of this performed incompetence, the song draws our attention to the question of commerce. Wun-Hi's occupation as a "small businessman" is as important to his stock character as his linguistic (and musical) infelicities. One negative interpretation that could be drawn from the situation is that while Wun-Hi may be assimilated with respect to his work—a merchant like any other—his musical-verbal nature suggests that he will never truly be "Western/British/American." On the other hand, the play's structure depends on treating the Japanese characters as figures subordinate to but much more allied with the British characters; Wun-Hi then becomes the figure most likely to carry the negative stereotypes of Asian people; he is the scapegoat whose comic abjection allows the other interracial exchanges to be tolerated. Although the basic structure of prejudice is left intact, in other words, its lines of demarcation may be able in the right circumstances to shift, however slightly, toward greater inclusiveness.

Inevitably, the ethnic songs that focused on more recent immigrant ethnic groups referred back to minstrelsy for their primary strategies of masquerade. And at the turn of the century, minstrelsy, though greatly transformed from its earlier historical incarnations, had in no way vanished. In the hands of especially gifted performers, "coon songs" of many types could carry substantial sub- and countertexts in performance, ones that ironized the manifest stereotyping that was probably a requirement for any performance at all. The legendary team of Bert Williams and George Walker, who for a stretch of time billed their act as "Two Real Coons" (as opposed to the white folks who were obviously faking it), were famous for their subtle ways of transforming the conventions of minstrelsy in their routines. One of their great performances came in the 1901 show *Sons of Ham*, a comedy in which the two play hoboes who drift into Denver, Colorado, where they are mistaken for the long-lost children, home at last from boarding school, of a rich man named Ham. But then they learn that Ham's real sons, away trying to become acrobats, are about to return. More hilarity ensues. The songs contained in this musical range over topics familiar in minstrel shows, but many of the most standard racial clichés are either omitted from the action or noticeably undermined by aspects of the performance.

The love song "My Little Zulu Babe," for instance, was recorded by Williams and Walker in 1901, the year of the show's run.[13] There are a number of features worth noting, all having to do with the strikingly idiosyncratic way that the duo treat it. First, almost the only words that are completely clear in the recording are those of the (white) announcer giving the song's title and the performers' names. The sonic surface becomes a good deal murkier in what follows, and this is not entirely the result of the recording technology that was used. Williams, who is singing lead, employs a strong minstrel-show accent difficult for modern listeners to decipher, and his joyously

messy singing, chock-full of vocal breaks, slides, and muf-
fled syllables, masks the lyrics even further. Careful listening,
however, reveals some details of what is present, as well as
what is not: the song describes the charms of the eponymous
"little Zulu babe," who lives "beside the Nile" (not geograph-
ically coherent, but good enough for a vaudeville audience
c.1900), as well as the singer's determination to propose and
celebrate the wedding in her town. What is *not* present are
all the typical verbal markers of African primitiveness—aside
from the surrounding "jungle," there is nothing particularly
exotic in the lyrics of the song to place the Zulu maiden in
a stereotyped position. Instead, Williams's performance can
be taken as making him into something of a "fool for love."
The comedy of his delivery is vastly amplified by Walker's
background clowning: he interjects an assortment of wails,
yodels, and other "jungle noises" into the background, son-
ically painting a cartoonish stylization of the Zulu babe's
surroundings—but not of her (◉ Example 6.3). And given
that Williams is so audibly in on Walker's jokes, it may raise
the question of just whom the joke is ultimately on. In fact,
this kind of slippery humor was the norm for the routines
that Williams and Walker had developed and in part accounts
for the enormous influence that Williams, especially, had on
comedians black and white alike.

These three songs, taken together, touch on some of the
entanglements of racial and ethnic types as they appeared in
New York performances. In a way, stock characterizations in
these songs may be thought of as analogous to genres as defined by the formal properties of the music and lyrics: that is,
these stereotypes set up a generalized set of characteristics that
not only act as a container for the specifics of a given performer
but also create a horizon of expectations in the audience. To the
extent that we are conversant with a given set of conventions,
we will be primed to look here, not over there; to hear this, not

that. But at the very moment that conventions are stabilized, they become newly available for productive contradictions. This kind of stereotyping did not vanish with the spread of recording and the erosion of vaudeville, though it did begin to recede from the extremely blunt forms it took in the nineteenth century. One of the things its practical usage handed down to later Tin Pan Alley composers, however, was a sense that the artifice of a song was, after all, one of its major potential virtues.

TIN PAN ALLEY AND BROADWAY BEFORE WORLD WAR II

The first significant reference to a "Golden Age" of the American musical—a term that has now come to refer, most often, to the two decades or so before the mid-1960s—was by Gerald Bordman, who continues to locate this era between 1924 and 1937, coincident with the years George Gershwin was most active as a composer for Broadway and Tin Pan Alley. In being the first to apply this term to the musical, Bordman both claims a valuable history for Broadway and asserts a specific period of arrival, during which the tug of war between operetta and more distinctively American styles sorted itself out, generally in favor of the latter.[14] It was during this period that the "standard" 32-bar Tin Pan Alley type of song fully established itself, a type that accommodated all of the Tin Pan Alley venues and markets mentioned above, including not only Broadway, but also Hollywood, jazz, sheet music, recording, and radio. For Bordman, implicitly, the basis for this Golden Age was song, the element that placed all of these markets and venues (most importantly for Bordman, revues and book shows) in the same plane of existence, so that the relative value and impact of shows could be judged mainly by their songs and their effectiveness in putting those songs across.

The mature American musical emerged from the interweaving of, and competition between, two separate strands of theatrical music-making: adapted European operetta traditions (mainly English and Viennese) and a number of traditions that shared the practice of staging popular song, deriving in part from the English music hall and similar traditions. Tin Pan Alley—which, like the studio system in Hollywood with respect to film, grew to control the marketplace of song in America—grew up alongside the musical in New York, both literally and figuratively, and they long maintained a closely symbiotic relationship. Many date the beginnings of Tin Pan Alley to the spectacular success of Charles K. Harris's "After the Ball," a song interpolated into the touring version of *A Trip to Chinatown* in 1892. But Tin Pan Alley's connection to theatrical Broadway predated that success, as is clear from the way Tin Pan Alley followed the theatrical district as it migrated north from its earlier center near Union Square (East 14th Street), to 28th Street in the 1890s, and eventually to the Brill Building near Times Square, built in 1931. The term itself was coined by Monroe H. Rosenfeld in the 1890s in reference to its 28th Street iteration, but the classic "Tin Pan Alley" song emerged only in the 1920s and '30s with the generation of songwriters headed by Irving Berlin, George Gershwin (especially with his brother Ira as lyricist), Jerome Kern (with Oscar Hammerstein II and others), Cole Porter, and Richard Rodgers (with Lorenz Hart).

The musical styles and forms of Tin Pan Alley, while always responsive to the needs of the musical stage, also played to a popular marketplace, following a line of development from nineteenth-century waltz songs to ragtime and "Coon" songs in the early twentieth century, to later styles derived from jazz, at all times maintaining as well a spread from sentimental (maintaining a dual allegiance to the parlor-song tradition and operetta) to humorous and more rhythmically inflected songs. Both onstage and in the marketplace, songs also played to a wide variety of topical interests, including, as discussed, a now-discomfiting engagement with ethnic, racial, and gendered stereotypes. Their use of dance rhythms and styles, too, pointed toward a need for songs to succeed on many fronts, whether by making them easier to put over onstage, allowing them to serve as a vehicle for social dance, or helping them to catch on with the public as songs to be sung at home, where they might also be listened to (and possibly danced to) through radio or recordings.

The vast majority of Tin Pan Alley songs use a verse-chorus structure, in which the "verse" either narrates a story or establishes a dramatic situation, and the "chorus" either acts as a punctuating refrain or represents the song promised by the dramatic setup. While the narration-refrain type was more typical in Tin Pan Alley's first generation (e.g., in the classic waltz-song, such as "After the Ball," or in the ragtime-song, such as Bob Cole and J. Rosamund Johnson's "Under the Bamboo Tree" of 1902), the "dramatic situation" song type came to dominate in the 1920s, employing the "classic" Tin Pan Alley 32-bar form for the chorus. While in both types, broadly speaking, the refrain or chorus would have been understood as the "song itself," the dependency on the verse lessened considerably as the new type evolved, a development that served all relevant marketplaces and venues.

Charles K. Harris's "After the Ball" offers a good example of how the earlier type worked, employing a relatively lengthy narrative verse and relatively short refrain (as compared to the later type). The song's full narrative takes three verses to unfold, and it is only with the third iteration of the refrain-chorus that we fully understand that the singer-narrator's early jealousy and rebuke have in time turned to regret tinged with self-reproach. The success of the song depended both on the dramatic arch of its verse-based narrative and the memorable chorus, during which, in public performance, or while listening to radio or recordings, auditors might join in, enjoying the waltz-based lilt of the "After" that opens each of the first few lines, and savoring the wistful "feminine" endings on the key words "over," "leaving," "aching," and "vanished." The refrain thus presents a sonic image of the ball as a metaphor for the "vanished" promise of married bliss, a combination that became even more effective as the waltz-song, as a type, evolved into an emblem of nostalgia (● Example 6.4).[15]

By 1927, indeed, this transition of the older type was officially complete. That year's *Show Boat*, in one of a handful of period musical references, brings in "After the Ball" as an emblem of the 1893 Chicago Fair, along with Sousa's "Washington Post March" and Broadway imitations of both spirituals and blues ("Ol' Man River" and "Can't Help Lovin' Dat Man"; ● Example 6.5; ● Example 6.6), the last two presented as a kind of African American "roots" music. In other ways, too, *Show Boat* positions itself as a kind of "threshold" show. Produced with extravagant staging by Florenz Ziegfeld, renowned impresario of the Ziegfeld Follies, *Show Boat* was originally to have included a mini-revue in the second act performed by Paul Robeson (who rejected the idea, and the role of Joe in the bargain, although he joined the show later and would become closely identified with "Ol' Man River").[16] In other ways, too, the show seems poised between operetta and revue, superimposing them in a way that was potentially (and in the long run, actually) transformative. In making life along the Mississippi the site of operetta-based nostalgia and intrigue, it also constructed a space to celebrate an African American musical heritage and gave that heritage an onstage, dramatic presence, where it is valued both through nostalgia and as a revitalizing presence, without (in the context of its era) over-sentimentalizing the role of blacks in the postwar

South. Often thought of as the first classic "book" musical, *Show Boat* is equally important for completing the transition, on Broadway, from European operetta to American operetta, in the process effacing operetta as such by replacing its European musical core with an African American–styled musical panorama, encompassing spirituals, blues, characteristic dance, and ragtime (the latter oddly positioned as a white appropriation). It is this successful stylistic superimposition, along with *Show Boat*'s unprecedented success in revivals, that lends plausibility to the claim that it marks the beginning of the American musical's maturity as a genre.

But if *Show Boat* may be understood as a kind of new beginning, it remains unclear what exactly it might be seen to have either launched or displaced. In Bordman's configuration of the Golden Age (1924–37), *Show Boat* is but part of the broader emergence of a new kind of song that blended styles in a characteristic American way, and he is probably right to date this emergence back to 1924, when Gershwin began to enjoy real success on Broadway (although his ending with Gershwin's untimely death in 1937 seems a bit overdramatic, especially since Cole Porter's star was then emphatically in the ascendant). But the continued success of the new style being developed by Gershwin, Berlin, Kern, and others during the mid-1920s and its easy transitions among venues and markets did not depend on what many historians have seen as the revolutionary aspect of *Show Boat*: its vaunted position in the evolution of the integrated book musical—which somehow had to wait until *Oklahoma!* sixteen years later to receive a sustainable echo. In light of this traditional if misguided focus, it is important to note both that *Show Boat*'s integrated book is scarcely unique for its time (although its durability in revivals is), and that it is the song type itself that truly mattered to audiences of the day. In this we may concur with Bordman, for it was indeed song that sustained *Show*

Boat and countless other shows and films of the era, whatever their level of integration.

"NATURAL" FORM VERSUS "FORMULA"

In the second half of the Tin Pan Alley era, when the style developed an even closer connection to the Broadway stage while remaining the source of America's most popular music (roughly the 1920s through the mid-1950s), a number of factors combined to shift the form and expressive strategies of the basic song-type. Technology (especially radio and recording) imposed increasingly stringent demands on the length of a song. More subtly, the fecundity of the genre as a basis for jazz improvisations and arrangements, as well as for extended dance sequences, tended to dictate a standard, moderate-length formal structure, functioning much like binary forms in the eighteenth century. And while earlier Tin Pan Alley songs played into practices of song-interpolation, later types had to fit into particular dramatic moments, as what may be termed "fragments of expressivity" (Knapp, *National Identity*, 77–78). These forces conspired to shape the form and the potential of the song in fundamental ways and made its 32-bar form the standard for the type (although for many venues the 12-bar blues form, sometimes crossbred with the 32-bar form, worked at least equally well).

This standardization of 32-bar song form, however, has always had its detractors, who have used it and other recurring features of the Tin Pan Alley song to decry its "formulaic" aspect. Certainly there are songs from this era that seem formulaic, and to their detriment. But it is entirely possible to be thoroughly formulaic—that is, to employ formulas at nested lower levels within the basic 32-bar formula—and still engage listeners freshly, often through a deft deployment of lyrics. Cole Porter's "list" songs, such as "You're the Top" or "Anything Goes" (both from *Anything Goes*, 1934), provide ready examples. But the formulaic can serve aesthetic functions beyond humor; even in these "list" songs, the formula-driven humor deflects and disconcerts, cloaking the expression of genuine feeling with crucial deniability. More broadly, formulas may create a sense of containment for what might otherwise seem emotionally risky or impart a sense of naturalness or inevitability to what might otherwise seem strange or unlikely, in these and other ways lending ontological conviction to content that might not otherwise persuade. More subtly, and surprisingly often—surprising, that is, for those who have bought into the negative profiling of Tin Pan Alley as formulaic—creating a sense of a well-known formula can lull listeners into a sense of occupying a familiar, "natural" space, so that they might not notice how unformulaic things actually are within that space. Examples range from the structural freedom of the formula itself, to specific devices that deflect strict formula in one way or another, and to deft uses of formula to manage a potentially disruptive element, be it harmonic, melodic, or rhythmic.

To begin with, 32-bar form is not a single formula but an array of conventions, generally resulting in four balanced phrases of eight bars each, or an easily recognized variant of this arrangement (involving, for example, cadential extensions). The most common design includes two repetitions of the first phrase separated by a contrasting phrase (often referred to as the "bridge," "release," or "middle eight"), resulting in an AABA thematic structure—a design, often termed "song form," with a pedigree dating back to the eighteenth century. Somewhat less common is a two-part structure, ABAB, evoking "binary" or "period" structures, also standardized in the eighteenth century. In either type, the final phrase might be varied significantly (thus, AABC or ABAC); indeed, variations of material in repetition are quite common, so long as the gesture of repetition—and of returning, as if inevitably, to the familiar—is clear. Typically, an extension of the form in performance will include an instrumental interlude, sometimes danced, followed by a final repetition of the concluding phrase (thus, AABA *B* A, where the second B is performed instrumentally and the final two "A" phrases are identical).

Within the conventions of 32-bar form, the apparently formulaic can disguise some surprising departures. The familiar song "Always" (Berlin, 1925) flirts with each of the formal types identified above but follows none of them, resulting in a form that might best be described as ABCD, while nevertheless providing a secure sense of balances maintained or restored, especially through its repetitions of the title word. Remarkably, "Always" thus imparts an extraordinary sense of comfort while surreptitiously violating most of the basic expectations of the form. And using a device shared with a few other songs, "Oklahoma!" (from *Oklahoma!*, 1943), doubles the basic dimensions of the form (16-bar phrases instead of 8-) while keeping to an 8-bar bridge ("We know we belong to the land . . ."), thus seeming to follow convention while heightening the song's sense of expansion through an internal contrast in phrase proportions.

As in "Always," the gesture of repetition in Tin Pan Alley songs is often deflected without disrupting the basic gesture, in some cases adding a patina of urgency or mystery and in others expressively shifting emphasis. "My Funny Valentine" (Rodgers and Hart, from *Babes in Arms*, 1937), for example, moves a third upward at the beginning of the second "A" phrase, angling toward the relative major (which arrives with the bridge). The final "A" phrase then moves through both keys at its outset, completing a process that adds crucial expressive energy and leads to an ending in a different key from the opening, all accomplished within phrases that will seem to be unproblematic repetitions to most listeners (🔊 Example 6.7). Another device used in "Funny Valentine"—reaching a higher pitch with each repeated phrase—is used in many songs of this era (such as "Ol' Man River") and especially favored by Cole Porter, who used it, for example, in "All through the Night" and "I Get a Kick Out of You" from *Anything Goes* (1934; the latter song from 1931), and "So in Love" from *Kiss Me, Kate* (1948)—which, like "My Funny Valentine," ends in a different key from the opening. All of these songs employ the device with considerable subtlety, but "All through the Night" is particularly deft in its coordination of unpredictable upward leaps that spring free of the song's sagging chromatic lines to give additional emphasis to key words: "close *to me . . . You* and your love" (🔊 Example 6.8).

While all of these devices preserve a *sense* of the formulaic while departing from actual formula, this kind of balance between order and disruption is probably never so crucial as with "rhythm" songs, a type of Tin Pan Alley song that employs a potentially disruptive (and often hard to sing) "hook" that is then contained within the strict phrasing dictated by the type. "Fascinating Rhythm" (George and Ira Gershwin, from *Lady Be Good*, 1924), "Puttin' on the Ritz" (Berlin, 1930, from the film of the same title), and "I Got Rhythm" (George and Ira Gershwin, from *Girl Crazy*, 1930) are three well-known "rhythm" songs that all lead with their distinctive and disruptive hooks and then depend on the 32-bar form to restore a controlling stability.

The hook for "Fascinating Rhythm" is an insistent melodic pattern of six eighth-notes followed by an eighth-note rest, yielding a three-and-a-half-beat pattern that pulls backward against the bar line, driven by the shifting accentual patterns of the lyric; briefly stabilized in the fourth iteration, the pattern is then repeated at a higher pitch level for the second half of the "A" phrase within an ABAC structure (▶ Example 6.9). The device in "Puttin' on the Ritz" is similar but paced more slowly; its seven-beat melodic structure (including an awkwardly placed syncopation) is sorted out, within each "A" phrase of an AABA structure, through a measured pause and a more straightforward presentation of the title phrase (⊙ Example 6.10). "I Got Rhythm" places its title phrase within its rhythmic hook, a thrice-repeated, evenly spaced four-note phrase that cuts across the basic rhythm by virtue of its consisting entirely of dotted quarter-notes, starting off the beat and thus imposing a slower rhythm that coincides in alignment with its background only on the third syllable of each iteration ("I got *rhy*-thm"; ⊙ Example 6.11). Interestingly, the rhythmic hook in each of these "formulaic" songs has a different significance; in "Fascinating Rhythm" it is imposed from without, as something (ostensibly) unwelcome that takes hold of the singer, whereas in "Puttin' on the Ritz" it reflects the inner awkwardness of described behavior (allied in its first version with an imputation of racialized difference)[17] and in "I Got Rhythm" it betokens a mastery of something difficult—even if more singers fail than succeed in rendering its rhythmic device accurately.

"EQUIPMENT FOR LIVING"

According to the scholar Philip Furia, the vast majority of Tin Pan Alley songs published during the 1920s and '30s were love songs.[18] In fact, during these decades questions of sexual desire and identity had become central to many understandings of modernity, especially among the bohemian crowd in New York City, whose elaborate participation in the artistic avant-garde (at this point, closely connected with many aspects of popular culture, particularly music) gave their widely publicized interpretations of modern love tremendous influence.

The advent of medical sexology in the late nineteenth century, for instance, had presented a painstakingly constructed taxonomy of sexual "dysfunctions"—which, ironically, offered the subjects under classification an opportunity to appropriate the medical labels, enabling a bewildering host of possible sexual identities.[19] The related discourse of psychoanalysis had placed questions of sexuality and its pervasive but hidden manifestations at the center of human subjectivity; not only was sexual content potentially everywhere, but there was also a much-expanded vocabulary with which to discuss it. Freud and his circle favored the rhetoric of science in presenting their account of sexuality as well, giving psychoanalysis the progressive luster of biology, chemistry ("yeah, chemistry"), and above all physics.

No less important were shifts in propriety and the laws that underwrote it. In the wake of nineteenth-century feminist actions such as the suffrage movement and the battles for access to birth control and family planning, and equal access to education, the protocols of feminine respectability began to shift and broaden considerably; in so doing, they revised the protocols of masculine respectability, as well. Modernist art movements, which placed challenges to bourgeois morals and tastes at the center of many projects, constantly challenged normative assumptions about what could and could not be explicitly represented—the best evidence of this in the United States was the obscenity proceedings brought against Gautier's *Mademoiselle de Maupin* (1922), Hall's *The Well of Loneliness* (1929), and, most famously, Joyce's *Ulysses* (1933). In each case, notions of artistic merit and "scientific" exploration contributed significantly to the arguments against censorship. And in the United States, these shifts in style took place within the milieu of Prohibition, which rather than elevating public morals by banning alcohol contributed to a widespread cynicism about all moral legislation.[20]

The effective collapse of the older models of gender, especially among the influential urban classes of America, meant that the protocols of love and courtship that helped realize those models quickly seemed out of date; but there were no alternative structures of affection and romance that would replace them. Instead, an array of possible models took the place of the old erotic regime; at the same time, the representation of modes of courtship became one of the major concerns of Tin Pan Alley songs. And so, by way of a conclusion to this chapter, we briefly consider a few points related to this development in two songs from Tim Pan Alley's Hollywood mode.

The 1932 musical *Gay Divorce* was Fred Astaire's last Broadway show before moving to Hollywood. Of the ten or twelve songs Cole Porter provided for the production, only one—"Night and Day"—survived the show's transformation into the 1934 film *The Gay Divorcee*.[21] Although the film alters elements of the scanty plot, it keeps the essential structure of a screwball comedy, in which a divorce sought out of boredom, faked adultery, a barely covertly gay gigolo, mistaken identity, and so on combine to comment lightheartedly on the travails of modern marriage. But "Night and Day" itself, though an elegant display of verbal and musical wit, takes courtship quite seriously. The terms in which it does so are apparent in the performance by Fred Astaire as he sings to Ginger Rogers. The song's verse sets up a series of similes that concatenate the primitive (jungles, tom-toms—a clear reference to jazz) with the technological (the clock) and nature (rain). The musical setting is melodically a chant-like reciting tone—Porter was well known for tailoring his songs to the capacities of specific performers, and in this case he had in mind Astaire's limited vocal range but also his sensitive phrasing and diction—not to mention his talent as a dancer. The repeated pitches, while they suit Astaire's skills well, also immediately start to establish an obsessive quality to the song's notions of courtship. It is also significant that, although the verse at first projects a steady rise in pitch level, suggesting urgency, just before the turn into the refrain the melody relaxes back to its initial pitch. Taken together with the refrain's propensity for gracefully drooping gestures, the melody establishes a fascinating tension between the suave wistfulness of possibly unrequited love and the thrum of underlying passion. As for the lyrics of the refrain, it is difficult to decide whether the omnipresence of the first person—the song is fundamentally not a set of compliments, as might be expected in romance, but instead a brilliant set of self-descriptions—is the result of tact or narcissism. If it is a plea for affection, then it is one that avoids ever making an outright proposition (⏺ Example 6.12).

Shall We Dance, released in 1937, was the seventh film featuring Fred Astaire and Ginger Rogers. Unlike *The Gay Divorcee*, it did not start as a stage musical: it arose from RKO's decision to create its own version of Rodgers and Hart's *On Your Toes*. The Gershwins were persuaded to sign on for what would be their first Hollywood musical. Again, courtship and marriage play a central role. In this case, the romantic leads, who are from different worlds (ballet and tap), are thrown together in a stunt marriage but gradually realize that what started out as a ploy has become "real." George Gershwin was reportedly excited about the opportunity to compose in a range of dance styles, and the score is stylistically quite rich. "They Can't Take That Away from Me," one of the film's most popular numbers, is a foxtrot, and its mode of courtship is complementary to that outlined in "Night and Day." That is, "They Can't Take That" is a not a self-description but a very detailed set of compliments. The beloved's style—clothes, hair, gestures—are listed as examples of the persistence of memory—and in this case, the repeated pitches in the melody (Gershwin's own acknowledgment of Astaire's particular skills?) becomes less a sign of romantic obsession and more a jaunty launching pad for the affectionate listing of details (⏺ Example 6.13).

Such short descriptions barely brush on the range of ways that Tin Pan Alley songs offered vehicles and models for constructing styles of courtship, but they nevertheless suggest how we might heighten our sensitivity to the kind of cultural work they participated in. In the authentistic moods of Cold War America, the stylish impersonality of such songs fell under suspicion: where was the truth of the performer's experience in a frothy commercial love song? But to a significant extent, many of the cultural battles fought in the United States over the last few decades have been less about "truth" and more about "impression management." They have in important ways been about negotiating a system of manners that we can collectively tolerate. Within this realm, it may be that Tin Pan Alley, with its elaborate romantic ad hocs, can offer us insights into our present as well as our past.

NOTES

1. The most important of these were Lederer's *The Passing Show*, Hippodrome "Extravaganzas," the Music Box "Revues," the "Grand Street Follies," the "Greenwich Village Follies," the "Garrick Gaieties," "Artists and Models," Earl Carroll's "Vanities," and George White's "Scandals."
2. See Gerald Bordman, *American Musical Theatre: A Chronicle*, 3rd ed. (New York: Oxford University Press, 2001) and http://www.ibdb.com
3. See Rose Rosengard Subotnik, "Shoddy Equipment for Living? Deconstructing the Tin Pan Alley Song," in *Musicological Identities: Essays in Honor of Susan McClary*, ed. Steven Baur, Raymond Knapp, and Jacqueline Warwick (Aldershot, UK: Ashgate, 2008), pp. 205–18.
4. "Tenement" in this sense refers to cheaply built structures, often without adequate plumbing or ventilation, into which vast numbers of impoverished immigrants were crowded. The disastrous

condition of the buildings and consequences for their inhabitants were a central concern for journalistic and political reformers— the New York State Tenement House Act of 1901, which corrected problems in the predecessor laws of 1867, 1879, and 1887, was the result of vigorous campaigning by the Progressive Movement of the turn of the century.

5. For the rest of this discussion the term "ethnic" will also stand in for "racial." To be sure, the differences between these two sets of characteristics can be understood as quite different—"race" is commonly held to be fixed to a degree that "ethnicity" is not. But especially since we are dealing with a period in which scientistic theories of "race" typically blended into considerations of what we would call "ethnicity," and since "race" as a term carries a much heavier load of historical sedimentation, we opt for "ethnic" as the more easily generalized term.

6. Jacob A. Riis, *How the Other Half Lives: Studies among the Tenements of New York* (New York, 1890; reprinted New York: Kessinger Publishers, 2004); online at www.authentichistory. com/1865-1897/progressive/riis/index.html, accessed November 4, 2010.

7. Nora Bayes, "How Can They Tell That Oi'm Irish?" (Norworth/ Bayes), recorded August 11, 1919 (78 Vic 700030 [mx C-9633-3]).

8. Husband #2 was the popular vaudevillian Jack Norworth (who co-authored the song under discussion); #3 was a dancer by the name of Harry Clarke; #4 was a New York businessman named Arthur Gordon.

9. "Astarita" is a thinly disguised jest at the Astors; "Vandergould" manages to send up the Vanderbilts.

10. *The Geisha*, music by Sidney Jones, lyrics by Harry Greenbank, book by Owen Hall; additional songs by Lionel Monckton and James Philip. In fact, the musical was even successful in continental Europe. The show was one of a sequence of so-called Gaiety musicals that made up a substantial share of the British shows successfully trans-Atlanticized at the turn of the century.

11. James T. Powers, "Chin Chin Chinaman" (Jones/Greenbank), recorded December 5, 1898 (78/Berliner 525-X).

12. These are actually genuine difficulties for some Chinese speakers who learn English as a second language. If learning went in the

other direction, surely native Chinese speakers would be amused by English speakers' probable mismanagement of Sinic tonal systems. Once again, the problem is not the presence of such speech challenges between languages but their reductions to a symbol of maladroit Otherness. In "Yinglish" theater, such bumps in language shift are a major resource for witty wordplay.

13. Bert Williams and George Walker, "My Little Zulu Babe" (Potter), recorded August 11, 1901 (78 Vic 1086 [mx 1086]).

14. Bordman's *American Musical Theatre* has been expanded, corrected, and updated several times since its first edition in 1978, with an expanded edition in 1986, a second edition in 1992, and a third edition in 2001; all versions include, as "Act IV," a chapter headed "The Golden Age of the American Musical, 1924–1937."

15. For more detailed discussions of this song and several others discussed in this chapter, see Raymond Knapp's *The American Musical and the Formation of National Identity* and *The American Musical and the Performance of Personal Identity* (Princeton, NJ: Princeton University Press, 2005 and 2006).

16. See Todd Decker, *Show Boat: Performing Race in an American Musical* (Oxford and New York: Oxford University Press, 2013).

17. The original version's racialized text was rewritten for Fred Astaire in the film *Blue Skies* (1946), and the later "cleaned-up" version is now standard.

18. Philip Furia, *The Poets of Tin Pan Alley: A History of America's Great Lyricists* (New York: Oxford University Press, 1990), p. 15.

19. Possibly one of the most striking examples of this occurs in Radclyffe Hall's famous lesbian novel *The Well of Loneliness*, in which the protagonist discovers her sexual identity by reading: she pages through Richard von Krafft-Ebing's famous classificatory work *Psychopathia Sexualis*, learning to call herself a lesbian in the process.

20. The liveliest generational social network in England during the 1920s was known as "the Bright Young People." Their attitudes and public styles closely resembled those of New York bohemia—not surprising considering how frequently the two worlds overlapped. For further information on this point, see

Mitchell Morris, "Lists of Louche Living: Music in Cole Porter's Social World," in *A Cole Porter Companion*, ed. Don M. Randel, Matthew Shafter, and Susan Froscher Weiss (Urbana, Chicago, and Springfield: University of Illinois Press, 2016), pp. 73–85.

21. The Hayes Office was troubled by the musical's original title, since it suggested that divorce was a happy occasion. Since the parties getting divorced, however, could be happy without upsetting the censors' sense of propriety (and perhaps persuaded by the parallel with *The Merry Widow*), the slight shift in title was accepted.

7

Integration

GEOFFREY BLOCK

■ □ ■

IN THE DECADES AFTER THE Supreme Court infamously ruled that separate could be equal (*Plessy v. Ferguson*, 1896), debates over racial integration in America gradually spread to a broader American public, fueled by W. E. B. Du Bois's and Booker T. Washington's forceful arguments. In popular culture, where race lines were contested by generations of performers and athletes, "integration" acquired more layers of meaning. Nearly sixty years after *Plessy*, another historic Supreme Court decision, *Brown v. Board of Education* (1954), overturned its predecessor and endorsed the ideal of racial integration, establishing a new national formulation of racial *veritas*: that separate is *not* equal. Integration—at least of public schools—became the law of the land.[1]

During the years between *Plessy* and *Brown*, the Broadway musical made its own tentative moves toward racial integration. In the epoch-making musical *Show Boat* (Jerome Kern and Oscar Hammerstein, 1927), audiences saw and heard two choruses, one black and one white, separately but equally powerfully, supporting a story that depicted the unfairness of laws against miscegenation. Moss Hart's and Irving Berlin's revue, *As Thousands Cheer* (1933), achieved its most poignant moment when Ethel Waters sang "Supper Time," a lament for her husband who had been lynched that day. Despite such forays into racial politics, however, "integration" on Broadway was, at least until the 1960s, an aesthetic aspiration largely unconcerned with racial politics. From the decades before *Brown* and continuing through the decades of its implementation, creators of the musical—Kern, Hammerstein, Rodgers, Lorenz Hart, Jo Mielziner, Agnes de Mille, Jerome Robbins, Boris Aronson, Hal Prince, Stephen Sondheim, and Michael Bennett, to name only a few pivotal figures—deliberately strove for an integration of the spoken, musical, danced, and scenic dimensions of a musical.

INTEGRATING THE MUSICAL PLAY

Shortly after the premiere of *Oklahoma!* (1943), Hammerstein compared his treatment of songs from that of its source play, Lynn Riggs's *Green Grow the Lilacs*:

> The songs we were to write had a different function. They must help tell our story and delineate characters, supplementing the dialogue and seeming to be, as much as possible, a continuation of dialogue. This is, of course, true of the songs by any well-made musical play. [2]

Six years after *Oklahoma!,* in his most detailed treatment on the art of lyrics, Hammerstein revisited his first show with Rodgers and the marriage between words and music, a key component of what he now calls "well-integrated," rather than "well-made." After sharing his belief that the musical expression of a story is comparable and equal to its verbal component, Hammerstein uses the word "integrated" to explain the merging of words and music "into a single expression":

> This is the great secret of the well-integrated musical play. It is
> not so much a method as a state of mind, or rather a state for two
> minds, an attitude of unity. Musical plays, then, are not "books"
> written by an author with songs later inserted by a composer and
> a lyric writer. [3]

Near the end of his long career, Rodgers too shared his thoughts
on the integrated musical in his autobiography:

> I have long held a theory about musicals. When a show works
> perfectly, it's because all the individual parts complement each
> other and fit together. No single element overshadows any
> other. In a great musical, the orchestrations sound the way
> the costumes look. That's what made *Oklahoma!* work. All the
> components dovetailed. There was nothing extraneous or for-
> eign, nothing that pushed itself into the spotlight yelling "look
> at me!" It was a work created by many that gave the impression
> of having been created by one. [4]

By the time Rodgers and Hammerstein's *Oklahoma!* launched
the so-called Golden Age in 1943, the principles of the "well-
integrated" (or "well-made") musical play, although not invariably endorsed or practiced, had become a widely recognized
and valued approach. The central characteristics of the "integrated" musical appear with ubiquity if not complete observ-
ance not only in *Oklahoma!* but also in many other critically
acclaimed shows.[5] From the quoted Hammerstein and Rodgers
passages, as well as from their musicals, we may glean the
following Principles of Integration (following each Principle is
an illustrative example or two from *Oklahoma!*):

1. *The songs advance the plot.* In "Surrey with the Fringe
   on Top," Curley improvises a seductive description of
   the surrey he plans to use to take Laurey to the box

social. Laurey and Aunt Eller become caught up in this extravagant idea, and by the end of the song—before it is interrupted by dialogue—the young couple have moved on to a deeper place in their still-unacknowledged but inevitable pairing.

2. *The songs flow directly from the dialogue.* By the time Ado Annie's beau Will Parker tells Aunt Eller, Ike Skidmore, and the assembled cowboys that he arrived in Kansas City "on a Frid'y," the song "Kansas City" has already begun. A little later Ado Annie explains to Laurey the problem she has with saying no, and within a line, dialogue has merged almost imperceptibly with music in "I Cain't Say No."

3. *The songs express the characters who sing them.* Ado Annie's "I Cain't Say No" expresses her flirtatiousness in language and music utterly foreign to Laurey. It would be equally implausible for Ado to address Will in a song remotely like Curley and Laurey's "People Will Say We're in Love" or a song as lush and romantic as Laurey's waltz "Out of My Dreams."

4. *The dances advance the plot and enhance the dramatic meaning of the songs that precede them.* Dance in *Oklahoma!* is exemplified by the historic dream ballet "Laurey Makes Up Her Mind," but the dancing that follows other songs is similarly "integrated" with the meaning of its companion song and the fabric of the show as a whole. For example, the dance styles discussed in the lyrics are executed in the dancing to "Kansas City," and Laurey's friends dance out the independence they extol in the words and music to "Many a New Day."[6] Similarly, dance in "The Farmer and the Cowman" expresses civilized engagement of the two groups, whereas "Oklahoma!" expands choreographically (and musically) to suggest the settling of an empty space by a growing population.

5. *The orchestra, through accompaniment and underscoring, parallels, complements, or advances the action.* In the reprise to "People Will Say We're In Love," it is the orchestra, not the singers, that initiates the musical development of this important dramatic moment, by underscoring the kissing and affectionate banter between Laurey and Curley with nearly half of the song's chorus. After that, Curley, in contrast to his behavior during this song in act I, welcomes full disclosure of their love ("Let people say we're in love"). (Along with the enhanced role of dance, the orchestra as a dramatic player will be exploited further in works such as *West Side Story* and *Sweeney Todd*.)

None of these Principles of Integration made a sudden appearance with *Oklahoma!* The integration of book and score was readily evident in the operettas of Gilbert and Sullivan, Johann Strauss, Jr., and Franz Lehár, all of whom had a major impact on Broadway from the late 1870s until World War I. The American musicals of Victor Herbert, especially *Naughty Marietta* (1910), also demonstrated some of the Principles of Integration common to European opera, operetta, and symphonic music. The integrated *musical* ideal was already for several generations also a common aesthetic component of both European symphonic literature from Beethoven to Mahler (known to musicologists as organic unity) and much opera, especially Wagner. But while this technique can contribute to the musical and dramatic integration of a work, an integrated musical, in the sense of the well-made musical play, does not require an organic score. In fact, when an organic score fails to imbue its organicism with dramatic meaning the result might be a *poorly* made musical play.

In an interview published four years before *Oklahoma!*, Rodgers insisted that songs in a show "must bear a family resemblance to the other musical material in the piece."[7] This is another way of endorsing the principles of musical organicism. Kern's organic approach to *Show Boat* and his use of such Wagnerian techniques as the grouping of themes within a larger family of motives, was recognized by Robert Simon in a contemporary profile of the composer in *Modern Music,* when he wrote that "themes are quoted and even developed in almost Wagnerian fashion."[8] In numerous musicals that followed *Show Boat,* including works by Rodgers and Hammerstein, Bernstein, Sondheim, and Lloyd Webber, organic musical scores constitute a key component of integration.

Among American-born Broadway practitioners Kern was perhaps the first to articulate the view that the well-made musical play should exhibit the dramatic values expected of well-made nonmusical dramas and comedies. A decade before *Show Boat* he expressed this position, in a 1917 interview:

> Plausibility and reason apply to musical plays as to dramas and comedies, and the sooner librettists and composers appreciate this fact the sooner will come recognition and—royalties. [9]

Later in this interview Kern demonstrated that some of his goals as a musical theater composer were identical to those later allied with the "integrated musical" of the 1940s:

> It is my opinion that the musical numbers should carry on the action of the play, and should be representative of the personalities of the characters who sing them. In a scene of college life you would never today present students in songs which deal with piracy or cheese manufacture unless the action of the piece demanded such activities. In other words, songs must be suited to the action and mood of the play.

Three years before *Show Boat,* the hugely popular operetta *Rose-Marie* (Friml and Hammerstein) not only contained a murder but also provided a demonstration of the future ideal, the integrated score:

> The musical numbers of this play are such an *integral* part of the action that we do not think we should list them as separate episodes. The songs which stand out, independent of their dramatic associations, are "Rosemarie," "Indian Love Call," "Totem Tom-Tom" and "Why Shouldn't We" in the first act, and "The Door of My Dreams" in the second act. [10]

A program note in Rodgers and Hart's *Chee-Chee* (1928) informed audiences that the short musical numbers "are so interwoven with the story that it would be confusing for the audience to peruse a complete list" (Rodgers 1975, 118). From *Show Boat* to *South Pacific* to *West Side Story* to *Sweeney Todd*, some musicals before and many musicals after *Oklahoma!* possessed integrated scores rich in thematic or "organic" unity.

Some integrated musicals are more integrated than others. Moreover, makers of musicals and their critics do not generally put forward the integrated musical as a polemical ideal but as a potentially profitable as well as an artistic approach (as Kern emphasizes) to a varied popular entertainment genre competing alongside a newer popular entertainment, the motion picture. To the extent that elaborate, coherent narratives were becoming the critical norm in Oscar-winning pictures such as 1939's incredible crop (including *Gone With the Wind* and the film musical *The Wizard of Oz*), musicals that are presentational rather than cinematic became less appealing as potential Hollywood crossover fodder.

Increasingly, scholars express the view that integration is actually present in musicals formerly dismissed for alleged incongruities between dialogue and song (in short, a perceived lack of integration). Even Cole Porter's perennially revived— and perennially revised—*Anything Goes* (1934), described by Raymond Knapp as the show that "seems to exemplify the pre-*Oklahoma!,* pre-'integrated' era of the American musical," contains songs that "are carefully situated within the show, often carrying important dramatic and thematic weight, and consistently setting out the characters' sensibilities and relationships in vivid, yet subtle, fashion."[11] Probing and substantial dramatic themes prominent in the integrated musical plays of Rodgers and Hammerstein (e.g., spousal abuse in *Carousel,* racial prejudice in *South Pacific*) also occur regularly in the 1930s musical, for example, *Of Thee I Sing* (1931), *Face the Music* (1932), *Johnny Johnson* (1936), *I'd Rather Be Right* (1937), and *The Cradle Will Rock* (1938), all of which challenge audiences with political and social satire rather than (or in addition to) romance.[12]

Before *Oklahoma!,* dances, when they followed a song, were considered more an accessory than an essential to the development of the story. Critics of nonintegrated dance numbers are prone to accuse such numbers of stopping the show, when in fact these glorious extraneous moments *are* the show. Nevertheless, prior to *Oklahoma!* dance gradually came to exert a stronger dramatic and plot-related presence. As early as the late 1920s, *New York Times* dance critic John Martin paid serious attention to the "prodigious raising of the level of the dancing" in Busby Berkeley's innovative choreography in Rodgers and Hart's *A Connecticut Yankee* (1927) and *Present Arms* (1928), including Berkeley's artistic way "of utilizing to the fullest extent the actual material which author and composer have provided for him."[13] Although the claim that George Balanchine's "Slaughter on Tenth Avenue" advances the action in *On Your Toes* (1936) has been challenged, the hybrid ballet hardly seems extraneous to a musical whose subject matter to a large extent concerns the reconcilable differences between ballet and jazz dance.

Film historian John Mueller emphasizes the importance of the "Night and Day" dance sequence to the integration in the

Broadway show *Gay Divorce* (1932), starring Fred Astaire, and soon thereafter in the Astaire and Ginger Rogers film adaptation with its less scandalous title, *The Gay Divorcee* (1934). For Mueller, "Night and Day" constitutes "the first of Astaire's major plot-advancing numbers in film, brought over from the stage play where it served a similar function," four years before "Slaughter on Tenth Avenue" and eleven before "Laurey Makes Up Her Mind."[14] In Mueller's view, Agnes de Mille's ballet "Laurey Makes Up Her Mind" from *Oklahoma!* enriches the plot but does not advance it. Such a position does not acknowledge that "Laurey Makes Up Her Mind" offered a dimension not present in *On Your Toes* or the integrated dancing of Fred and Ginger. More than simply advancing the plot, "Laurey Makes Up Her Mind" employs dance to vividly explore the psychological dimension of a central character in ways that dialogue and songs could not. Through dreams and nightmares, dance conveys Laurey's unspoken thoughts, unacknowledged sexuality, and fears that lie below the surface in her waking (and nondancing) state. The self-aware Ado Annie knows her mind; Laurey does not know hers until she has danced out her feelings in her dreams. Not even the remarkable integrated dances of Fred and Ginger try to accomplish so much.

While the demonstration of the Principles of Integration may be the exception rather than the norm before the 1940s, the principles appeared regularly and increasingly in shows from the 1910s through the late 1930s before the integrated ideal became the law for post-*Oklahoma!* aspirant musicals of the 1940s. In fact, the Princess Shows of Kern, Guy Bolton, and P. G. Wodehouse, Kern and Hammerstein's *Show Boat,* George and Ira Gershwin's *Of Thee I Sing* (book by George S. Kaufman and Morrie Ryskind), and George Gershwin's anomalous *Porgy and Bess* (book by DuBose Heyward, lyrics by Heyward and Ira Gershwin) are familiar pre-*Oklahoma!* realizations of the integrated ideal. In the far lesser known *Cat and the Fiddle* (1931)

Kern, in tandem with librettist-lyricist Otto Harbach, continued his efforts (according to the hype of its producer Max Gordon) "to work artistically and with greater integrity in the medium than may have been imagined" and "to make certain that there will be strong motivation for the music throughout."[15] As Stephen Banfield argues, the successful solution to a complex dramatic problem was to create "a plot and a treatment in which all the musical performances would be diegetic" (i.e., "music from an identifiable source within the fictional world of the film," a term increasingly applied successfully to musical theater studies).[16]

Toward the end of their long association, Rodgers and Hart in *Pal Joey* (1940) consistently used songs to explore character and enhance the story. *Lady in the Dark* (1941; book by Moss Hart, lyrics by Ira Gershwin, and music by Kurt Weill) used music dramatically to realize the dreams of its central character in a show that purposefully segregated nonmusical dialogue from continuous musical dreams. Significantly, contemporary reviews used the term "integrated" to describe what they saw and heard in these shows. It is not a term imposed by later historians and critics. The word "integration" does not, however, appear regularly in print until the arrival of *Oklahoma!*, after which it becomes ubiquitous.

First night *New York Times* reviewer Lewis Nichols, for example, wrote that "Mr. Rodgers's scores never lack grace, but seldom have they been so well integrated for *Oklahoma!*"[17] In a slightly later discussion of de Mille's choreography, John Martin described why he regarded the act I dream ballet so highly:

"Laurey Makes Up Her Mind" is a first-rate work of art on several counts. For one thing, it is so integrated with the production as a whole that it actually carries forward the plot and justifies the most tenuous psychological point in the play, namely, why

Laurey, who is obviously in love with Curly, finds herself unable
to resist going to the dance with the repugnant Jud. [18]

A couple of pages after Rodgers summarized "what made
Oklahoma! work" (see above), he acknowledged that "*Oklahoma!*
did, of course, have an effect on the musicals that came after it"
and that "everyone suddenly became 'integration'-conscious,
as if the idea of welding together song, story and dance had
never been thought of before." In refreshing contrast to most
musical theater historians (until relatively recently), Rodgers
offered a less grandiose claim for the epoch-making nature of
Oklahoma!, although he did see the work as innovative and
helpful to writers and composers looking for "a new incentive to
explore a multitude of themes and techniques within the framework of the commercial theater" (Rodgers 1975, 229).

As *Oklahoma!*'s innovations merged into the mainstream
of Broadway history, it has become increasingly common either to place the word "integrated" in quotes or to preface
integrated with the qualifier "so-called." In fact, straightforward use of the word "integrated" is probably the exception
in recent scholarship. In *The Musical as Drama* (2006), Scott
McMillin interprets the traditional book musical as inherently
non-integrated because of the sharply defined and incompat-
ible divisions between the normative book time (dialogue) and
the interruptions from number time (song). McMillin sees
the book and the score in *Oklahoma!* and musicals of the next
twenty or thirty years as separate and oppositional. As a prime
example he offers "People Will Say We're in Love" to illustrate
a nonintegrated song interruption of book time. McMillin
observes that some of the lyrics in this song do not truly fit the
characters who sing them (e.g., Laurey's lyrical reference to her
parents when in fact her parents are deceased), but he welcomes
the opportunity to hear from Curly and Laurey at this late stage
in act I even if the song does not advance the action.

The work of Stephen Sondheim demonstrates that it is possible to write "integrated" musical scores without paying allegiance to a Wagnerian ideal characterized by continuous orchestral underscoring beneath a through-sung melodic language that is neither recitative (sung speech) nor aria. For the most part, Sondheim maintains the formal distinctions common to the German singspiel, European and American operetta, and American musical comedies, with clear distinctions between dialogue and song. Unlike some works by Andrew Lloyd Webber, in Sondheim we usually have no trouble discerning the difference between musical speech and song. Even in a musical that exhibits the through-sung qualities of opera, such as *Sweeney Todd,* Sondheim offers considerable spoken dialogue, most noticeably at the climactic close of the work.[19] In Sondheim's *Sunday in the Park with George* (book and direction by James Lapine), the completion of Georges Seurat's painting at the end of act I also completes the musical ideas foreshadowed the moment he first faced his blank canvas. In *Into the Woods* (also with Lapine), the songs, like the intricate plot, derive from Jack's five-note "bean" theme, offer intricate motivic networks that are dramatically meaningful, and demonstrate the kind of organic unity that would be the envy of a Brahms symphony or Wagner opera.

. Before the 1970s, the integrated musical maintained the separate but equal conventions of book and number time. Sondheim, arguably Broadway's leading lyricist-composer of his generation, favored this separation over the less differentiated merging of the two dimensions found in later Verdi and Wagner and in many post-1970 Broadway musicals. Although Sondheim embraced organicism in some of his shows, he also has demonstrated a consistent antipathy toward opera:

> I don't like opera, but I have a feeling that I wish I did. Because, I'll tell you something, it's much more satisfying and easier to write

something like *Passion* than it is to write something like *Merrily We Roll Along*. To write a thirty-two-bar song that has freshness and style to it and tells the story is really hard. And nobody does it anymore. Everybody writes so-called "sung-through" pieces, and it's because anybody can write sung-through pieces. It's all recitative, and they don't develop anything, and it just repeats and repeats. And that's what most shows are. (Horowitz, 19–20)

CONCEPT

In the first "integrated" generation, despite the strong presence of choreographers (de Mille and Robbins) and directors (Rouben Mamoulian, Joshua Logan, George Abbott, George S. Kaufman, Moss Hart, and Robbins), composers and lyricists played a larger role than they would in a future era dominated by directors, choreographers, director-choreographers, and producers.[20] The controlling hand in the creation of *Oklahoma!* remained Rodgers and Hammerstein, not Mamoulian, despite the latter's distinctive and influential directorial stamp. In *Fiddler on the Roof* the primal roles of the librettist, lyricist, and composer were partly usurped by director-choreographer Robbins, to a far more visible extent than in *West Side Story*, where Robbins collaborated and grappled with two strong creative personalities, Arthur Laurents and Leonard Bernstein. In both *West Side Story* and *Fiddler*, Robbins's insistent question, "What is the show *about?*" led to major changes—for example, the replacement of a traditional opening number in *West Side Story* with an extended Prologue told entirely through dance. But *Fiddler* was more a Robbins show than its predecessor. After *Fiddler*, stagers had largely replaced librettists, lyricists, and composers as the dominant Broadway force.

West Side Story may have had dramatic meanings conveyed through song as well as dance, but *Fiddler on the Roof* also had a "concept," a central idea that governed the integration of the other dramatic elements (words, music, dance, and set design). To announce its presence, Robbins created an opening number in which the "concept," the breakdown of tradition, was made unequivocally clear and incarnate. Thereafter, the concept of tradition and its demise would occasionally reemerge during the course of the integrated book and number format, familiar from Rodgers and Hammerstein and Lerner and Loewe.

In the 1960s the idea of the "concept" musical thus began to replace "integration" as the critical encomium of choice, perhaps reflecting a broader social movement toward a modernist aesthetic that favored vision and subject matter to elaborate settings and narrative. As many musical theater historians have noted, the "concept" musical did not, however, first appear *ex nihilo* (or fully formed) in *Fiddler on the Roof* any more than the integrated musical made its debut with *Oklahoma!* Although with relatively short runs and seldom revived, Rodgers and Hammerstein's *Allegro* (1947) and Weill and Lerner's *Love Life* (1948) are well-known precedents, two earlier musicals organized around a central idea or concept. But the origins of the "concept" musical can also be traced back to loosely plotted revues organized around an idea such as newspaper headlines (*As Thousands Cheer*, 1933) or travel (*At Home Abroad*, 1935).

Two years after *Fiddler*, Hal Prince extended the "concept" musical to encompass elements of nonlinearity and extra-spatial dimensions in the "limbo" sections between reality and imagination in *Cabaret*. Since about half of *Cabaret* takes place outside of the Kit Kat Klub, however, the show as originally staged preserves the traditional book and number format. The metaphorical concept component—the cabaret as a metaphor for the moral decline of Germany that led to the rise of Hitler's

Third Reich—shared its conceptual space with the book and number time of non-cabaret scenes.

The 1972 film version of *Cabaret,* which earned Bob Fosse an Academy Award for direction, marked the end of an era that generally featured more faithful adaptations, an era significantly framed, as with the staged Golden Age musical, by the films of *Oklahoma!* (1955) and *Fiddler on the Roof* (1971). For the most part, film adaptations before *Oklahoma!*—which despite its general fidelity and completeness omitted a powerful and dramatic song from the stage version, Jud Fry's "Lonely Room"—typically rewrote the original book and treated the score, however integrated, as a dispensable item subject to significant cutting. To take one example out of many, the 1939 film adaptation of Rodgers and Hart's *Babes in Arms,* a show packed with hit songs in its Broadway staging, retained a total of two.

In contrast to the stage original, which included both book numbers and diegetic numbers, Fosse's filmed *Cabaret* takes a more realistic approach and reserves nearly all the musical numbers for the Kit Kat Klub (the exception is a public group singalong of "Tomorrow Belongs to Me" at an outdoor *Biergarten*). In general terms, film adaptations of Broadway musicals before 1955 for the most part increased realism without seeking to increase the integration of book and score. While film realism often produces imaginative, and sometimes surreal, results (e.g., the vaudeville routines growing out of Roxie's mind in the 2002 film adaptation of *Chicago*), the predilection for diegetic contexts generally leads to less rather than more integration of the musical's key component parts. On the other hand, the majority of film musical adaptations in recent years (*Dreamgirls, Hairspray, Mamma Mia!, The Phantom of the Opera, The Producers, Rent, Sweeney Todd*) have demonstrated a healthy tolerance for nonrealistic, even surrealistic, contexts for song and dance.

Four years after the staged *Cabaret,* Prince, along with
Sondheim and choreographer Michael Bennett, recentered the
role of the concept in the concept musical with *Company* (1970)
by including a less straightforward narrative line. Based on a
series of eleven one-act plays by George Furth, the musical's
amorphous plot leaves audiences unable to detect whether the
birthday gathering we see at the end of the show is the same
as the one that opens the show. In his autobiography, Prince
summarizes some of what made *Company* different from his
earlier work:

> *Company* was the first musical I had done without conventional
> plot or subplot structure. The first without the hero and heroine,
> without the comic relief couple. There are, of course, plots, but
> they are sub textual and grow out of subconscious behavior, psy-
> chological stresses, inadvertent revelations: the nature of the lie
> people accept to preserve their relationship. [21]

The characters in *Company* invade the space and the
number time of other characters and, in seeming contrast
to the "integrated" covenant between words and music,
many of the songs comment on the action or emotional
developments rather than grow directly from the dialogue
(some of the Kit Kat Klub songs in *Cabaret* had also served
as commentary). Concept in this sense opposes integration; since the plot is fundamentally nonlinear, the songs
cannot directly advance the plot. That said, in common
with the integrated musical, all the elements (words, music,
movement, and design) are interconnected and coalesce into
a unified whole. Furthermore, by the end of the show Robert
has grown as a character and has moved to a new *psychological* place in which he, like Laurey, makes up his mind
and embraces the meaning and responsibility of marriage
("Being Alive").

INTEGRATION REVISITED

James T. Patterson concludes, in his survey of race in America from the years after World War II until the mid-1970s, that for those opposed to segregation, *Brown v. Board of Education* "conveyed profound moral legitimacy to the struggle for racial justice, not only in the schools but also in other walks of life" (Patterson, 390). But not everyone in America at the time thought that school integration was in the best interests of all concerned. The politically conservative black writer Zora Neale Hurston questioned the wisdom of black children being forced to attend schools where they would be unwelcome, even endangered. Other critics objected to the presumption that black children in segregated schools would receive social damage and feel inferior in a black school of exceptional quality. The main criticism of *Brown*, which continues to the present, however, was its slow and dilatory implementation.

Naturally, parallels between the story of racial integration and the development and reception of the integrated musical can go only so far, and they occupy vastly different realms of sensibility. The differences and stakes were and remain separate and not at all equal. Nevertheless, some of the parallels are instructive. For example, although the integrated musical became the unwritten law of Broadway starting in the 1940s, the years after *Oklahoma!* witnessed successful if less spectacular runs of more "segregated" shows, such as *Mexican Hayride* and *Follow the Girls* (both in 1944). Despite its great score and canonic status, the integration of the subplot in *Annie Get Your Gun* (1946) was so tenuous that its songs and the characters who sang them frequently vanished from revivals.

Furthermore, the integrated musical was not without its detractors—for example, the distinguished critics Eric Bentley and George Jean Nathan, neither of whom welcomed the integrated musical with its artistic complexities, seriousness of purpose, ambition, and dramatically meaningful themes. For Bentley, writing in 1954, "the best musicals at present are not those with the biggest intentions behind them but those with the simple virtues in them of singable tunes and sheer showmanship."[22] When comparing the current revival of *On Your Toes* with recent fare, Bentley preferred the old-fashioned show with its "breath of a less stuffy generation," and he agreed with James Thurber "that something was lost during the forties and early fifties" when the "cocky, satirical, devil-may-care philosophy" abundant in Rodgers and Hart's 1930s hit gave way to loftier approaches (Bentley, 192). Nathan, an early champion of the serious dramas of Eugene O'Neill and Sean O'Casey, felt that the Broadway musical merited its separate and unequal status. He defended Hammerstein's sentimentality (a critical judgment that became hard to shake after *The Sound of Music*) and Rodgers's relentless tunefulness, and appreciated their musicals not for their modernity or integration but because they knew their place in the theatrical hierarchy in which the "lighter stage occupies the same position in music that the cocktail does at the dinner table" (to whet "the appetite for the better things to come").[23]

Although it was possible after *Oklahoma!* for the integrated musical to merge with musical comedy (e.g., *Guys and Dolls* and *Gypsy*), the integrated musicals of Kern, Rodgers and Hammerstein, and Bernstein (*Candide* and *West Side Story*, if not *On the Town* or *Wonderful Town*), among others, favored more serious subjects and came to exhibit some of the musical complexities more frequently found in opera. Both Bentley and Nathan resented these attempts "to make the-musical-that-is-more-than-a-musical." Starting in the 1970s with the musicals of Prince and Sondheim and in the late 1970s and 1980s with the musicals of Lloyd Webber, Alain Boublil, and Claude-Michel Schönberg, many high-profile musicals continued to address serious dramatic subjects and to favor operetta or even opera over musical comedy. With the arrival of musicals such as *Les Misérables, The Phantom of the Opera, Miss Saigon,* and *Sunset Boulevard* in the 1980s and 1990s, musicals not only got more serious but also grew in size—hence the soubriquet, the "megamusical," or in Mark Grant's dismissive parallel with the McDonald's Big Mac hamburger, the "The Age of McMusicals" (Grant, 304–15).

Ironically, integration, when it came to musicals, could prove for some critics to be too much of a good thing. Scott McMillin has tried to replace the term "integration" with "coherence," believing it to be a more accurate term regarding musicals in the 1940s. As he, like Grant and other critics and historians, dismisses the so-called megamusical of the 1980s for its pretentions and over-reliance on technology "in order to preserve the illusion of a seamless whole," McMillin acknowledges that while Rodgers and Hammerstein fell short of integration, they had "mastered the principles of difference that formed the earlier musicals."[24] Although *Phantom* may have departed from these principles of difference to create a show he regarded as "pretentious and overblown," McMillin nonetheless is prepared to "see the logic of claiming that the drive for integration has finally been achieved in Lloyd Webber" (McMillin, 165). The problem remains, for many, that integration has evolved from an ideal to become a false god and a source of criticism and ridicule. Specifically, the increasingly through-sung integrated musical, with its abandonment of the separation between book and number, has in recent decades become thoroughly entwined with the mostly negative critical status of Lloyd Webber, an association that has diminished the positive view of critics, if not audiences, toward the integrated ideal. With the musical, the problem is not integration per se but that a musical too saturated with integration is more prone to a sameness that can result in dramatic meaninglessness (Block 2009, 394–95, 402–7). But this is not always the case. In the musicals of Sondheim the musically integrated score is invariably dramatically meaningful. And, as Wagner has demonstrated, it is possible for integration and the dramatically meaningful to coexist in through-sung opera, as well.

Phantom and *Les Misérables* constitute excellent examples of how the development of the integrated musical thwarted at least two of the five Principles of Integration presented near the outset of this chapter: "*The songs express the characters who sing them*" and "*The orchestra, through accompaniment and underscoring, parallels, complements, or advances the action.*" Both of these shows, extensively through-sung, use a relatively small repertoire of musical themes and motives and recycle these melodies continuously throughout the work, usually with new lyrics. The technique ensures unity and musical integration and provides opportunities to create new dramatic meanings for musical ideas. However—and this happens often, especially in the latter show—when characters (and their underscoring) in these musicals use each other's music without regard to the appropriateness of the appropriation, the increased integration is matched by decreased dramatic meaning.

Classic American musicals of the Golden Age between *Oklahoma!* and *Fiddler on the Roof* are not immune from the "devil-may-care philosophy" of a 1930s show such as *Anything Goes* or *On Your Toes,* the latter explicitly and the former implicitly favored by Bentley. A good example is the canonic classic *Kiss Me, Kate* (1948), lyrics and music by Porter and book by Sam and Bella Spewack. Despite its greater integration compared with *Anything Goes, Kate* ignores dramatic logic (in Fred's act II reprise of "So in Love," sung alone by Lilli in act I),[25] loses an opportunity for nuance when Porter presents his characteristic alternation between major and minor in both the *Shrew* numbers and the Baltimore numbers rather than confining this identifier to one group or another to distinguish the two (Block 1997, 184–85; 2nd ed. 221), and offers the show-stopping "Too Darn Hot" without even a fig leaf of an "integrated" rationale.

In his chapter on *Les Misérables,* Joseph P. Swain offers numerous telling examples of infelicities that plague the over-integrated musical, which collectively exceed the relatively un-noticeable violations of the Principles of Integration found in *Kiss Me, Kate*:

> While it may be reasonable for Jean Valjean to recall Fantine's death song ("Come to Me") at his own demise, there is no reason for Eponine to convert it to a torch song ("On My Own"). Similarly, to sing again the evocative, half-mournful, half-hopeful melody by which Bishop Myriel charges Jean Valjean to change his life as a sentimental reminiscence of the dead students in "Empty Chairs" is a waste of a precious resource, musical semantics. [26]

The ideal of integration in the Broadway musical, which includes the European imports of the 1980s and 1990s, led to the super-integrated musical that has generated a split between critical and popular acclaim. In both the social and artistic versions of integration, ideals have led to disillusionment and cast doubt on the viability of the concept. Yet, despite disappointment in how the histories of racial integration and Broadway integration played out, both areas of American life can still point to demonstrable gains. At long last, America has elected a black president. And, whatever combination of good or ill may be ascribed to the integrated ideal on Broadway, the American musical, with some notable contributions from across the pond, has maintained its status into the present as one of the most vigorous, entertaining, popular, and challenging art forms.

NOTES

1. James T. Patterson, *Grand Expectations: The United States, 1945–1974* (New York: Oxford University Press, 1996), pp. 375–406.

2. Oscar Hammerstein II, "In Re 'Oklahoma!': The Adaptor-Lyricist Describes How the Musical Hit Came Into Being" (*New York Times* [May 23, 1943]: 11).

3. Oscar Hammerstein II, "Notes on Lyrics," in *Lyrics* (Milwaukee: Hal Leonard Books, 1985, 3–48), p. 15.

4. Richard Rodgers, *Musical Stages: An Autobiography* (New York: Random House, 1975; repr. New York: Da Capo, 1995, 2000), p. 227.

5. Geoffrey Block, "The Broadway Canon from *Show Boat* to *West Side Story* and the European Operatic Ideal" (*Journal of Musicology* 11.4 [Fall 1993]: 525–44), pp. 525–26.

6. Ethan Mordden, *Beautiful Mornin': The Broadway Musical in the 1940s* (New York: Oxford University Press, 1999), p. 75.

7. Richard Rodgers, "How to Write Music in No Easy Lessons: A Self Interview" (*Theatre Arts* [October 1939]: 741–46, p. 743; reprinted in *The Richard Rodgers Reader*, ed. Geoffrey Block [New York: Oxford University Press, 2002], 261–65).

8. Robert Simon, "Jerome Kern" (*Modern Music* 6.2 [January–February 1929]: 20–25), p. 24.

9. Louis R. Reid, "Composing While You Wait" (*The Dramatic Mirror* [June 2, 1917]: 5).

10. Hugh Fordin, *Getting to Know Him* (New York: Ungar Publishing, 1977), pp. 55–56 [italics mine].

11. Raymond Knapp, *The American Musical and the Formation of National Identity* (Princeton. NJ: Princeton University Press, 2005), p. 89

12. Alisa Roost, "Before *Oklahoma!*: A Reappraisal of Musical Theatre during the 1930s" (*Journal of American Drama and Theatre* 16.1 [Winter 2004]: 1–35), p. 15.

13. John Martin, "The Dance: New Musical Comedy Talent" (*New York Times* [July 22, 1928]: Section 7, 6).

14. John Mueller, "Fred Astaire and the Integrated Musical" (*Cinema Journal* 24.1 [Fall 1984]: 28–40), p. 31.

15. Max Gordon, with Lewis Funke, *Max Gordon Presents* (New York: Random House, 1963), p. 147; quoted in Stephen Banfield, *Jerome Kern*. New Haven. CT: Yale University Press, 2006), p. 179.

16. Banfield, 179. The definition of "diegetic" is quoted from Steve Blandford, Barry Keith Grant, and Jim Hillier, *The Film Studies Dictionary* (London: Arnold, 2001), p. 67.
17. Lewis Nichols, "'Oklahoma!' a Musical Hailed as Delightful, Based on 'Green Grow the Lilacs,' Opens Here at the St. James Theatre" (*New York Times* [April 1, 1943]: 27). See also Tim Carter, *Oklahoma!: The Making of an American Musical* (New Haven, CT: Yale University Press, 2007), pp. 173–74.
18. John Martin, "The Dance: De Mille's Oklahoma" (*New York Times* [May 9, 1943]: Section 10, p. 6).
19. Banfield, 291–92; Mark Eden Horowitz, *Sondheim on Music: Minor Details and Major Decisions* (Lanham, MD: Scarecrow Press, 2003), pp. 125–26.
20. Mark N. Grant, *The Rise and Fall of the Broadway Musical* (Boston: Northeastern University Press, 2004), pp. 277–303.
21. Hal Prince, *Contradictions: Notes on Twenty-Six Years in the Theatre* (New York: Dodd, Mead, 1974), p. 149.
22. Eric Bentley, "The American Musical," in *What Is Theatre?* (New York: Athenaeum, 1968, 190–93), p. 191.
23. George Jean Nathan, *The Theatre in the Fifties* (New York: Alfred A. Knopf, 1953), p. 234.
24. Scott McMillin, *The Musical as Drama: A Study of the Principles and Conventions behind Musical Shows from Kern to Sondheim* (Princeton, NJ: Princeton University Press, 2006), pp. 170 and 165.
25. Geoffrey Block, *Enchanted Evenings: The Broadway Musical from "Show Boat" to Sondheim and Lloyd Webber* (New York: Oxford University Press, 1997; 2nd ed., 2009), pp. 227–29.
26. Joseph P. Swain, *The Broadway Musical: A Critical and Musical Survey* (Oxford: Oxford University Press, 1990; 2nd ed., Lanham, MD: Scarecrow Press, 2002), p. 404.

8

After the "Golden Age"

JESSICA STERNFELD
AND ELIZABETH L. WOLLMAN

■ □ ■

THE TERM "GOLDEN AGE" IS riddled with unfair assumptions. It implies a consensus about when the American musical theater reached its aesthetic and cultural pinnacle, as well as when it began its alleged decline, and idealizes the integrated musical—in which music, dance, and drama are melded seamlessly into an artistic whole—over all other musical theater styles. Further, the term "Golden Age" is used notoriously loosely: depending on which history one reads, Broadway's Golden Age began anywhere between (or even before) Kern and Hammerstein's *Show Boat* (1927) and Rodgers and Hammerstein's *Oklahoma!* (1943); the end is placed anywhere between the mid-1950s and late 1970s.[1] There are, further, historians for whom the term has an entirely different emphasis: Allen Woll, for example, describes the 1920s as the "Golden Age" of black musicals.[2] The highly subjective term is thus potentially applicable to a vast array of musical subgenres.

The phrase "After the Golden Age" is also inherently negative: it implies that any musical to have opened in recent decades is by nature of its chronology somehow less artistically important or culturally resonant than those that opened in the past. Such judgments often extend to audiences, whose collective taste is seen to have declined precipitously since 1960.[3] Despite a growing number of writings that demonstrate the cultural importance of various contemporary musicals, examine how musicals have developed in style and sophistication, and explore ways that musicals have been adapted to reach larger, newly international audiences, even some recent histories exhibit hostility toward any post-1960 musical not written by Stephen Sondheim.[4] His work—often described as dissonant, intellectual, challenging—is frequently contrasted with the blockbuster hits that came to be known as megamusicals. Epic in scope and staging, often featuring sung-through scores that draw on operatic and pop influences, and enormously popular with audiences, megamusicals such as *Les Misérables* (1987) and *The Phantom of the Opera* (1988) have had an enormous influence on the economy, audience, and reception of recent musicals in general.

While the term "Golden Age," for all its implications, is not ideal, its continued application is understandable. The American musical has undergone a number of monumental changes in recent decades, as a result of economic, technological, social, and aesthetic developments, all of which have affected the demands of a changing audience. Despite frequent insistence to the contrary, the American musical is not dead. But it is certainly different from what it was a half-century ago. Scholars who consider the contemporary musical must consider as well the many ways it has evolved. In the following pages, we discuss some of the more important developments that have affected the stage musical in the past half-century.

THE ECONOMICS OF PRODUCTION

Broadway has always been about making money: since musicals existed, there have been producers hoping to profit from them. In the early twentieth century, Broadway musicals were relatively inexpensive to mount, and most did not need to run for long to recoup investments. During the 1920s—Broadway's busiest decade—it was common for fifty or more musicals to open each season; even mildly successful ones spawned national tours.

The Great Depression and the advent of film both changed Broadway's economic landscape dramatically. Musical output after 1929 fell precipitously. The 1929–30 Broadway season offered only thirty-two new musicals; there would be only thirteen in the 1933–34 season (Bordman, 502, 534). In terms of quantity, Broadway would never bounce back: offerings would rise just slightly through the twentieth century, with only two seasons capping at twenty musicals.[5]

The amount of money needed to produce a musical has risen since the onset of the Depression, but especially since the 1960s. The cost of production, coupled with the introduction of several cheaper, more widely accessible entertainment forms, has forced the musical to struggle financially and aesthetically at various periods during the postwar era. Historians who argue that the so-called Golden Age ended in the late 1960s or early 1970s are likely associating the alleged stylistic decline of the musical with its economic struggles during this era.

The 1970s were problematic not only for the theater industry but also for New York City in general. Excessive spending by the city government through the 1950s and 1960s, combined with a declining stock market and period of stagflation in the early 1970s, caused New York to teeter toward bankruptcy by mid-decade. The economic slump exacerbated a slew of social ills that had plagued New York since the 1960s. Homelessness, drug abuse, and a sharp increase in crime had a profoundly negative impact on the city's image, and thus on tourism.

Socioeconomic woes were especially palpable in Times Square, which became a symbol of urban decay. The neighborhood's many "grinder" houses, porn shops, peepshows, and massage parlors—and the related rise of petty crime—alienated theatergoers, especially after the city fired 20,000 civil servants in 1975. Weak theater attendance, combined with skyrocketing inflation, forced producers to slash budgets while simultaneously boosting ticket prices. Through the early twentieth century, tickets for most Broadway shows were relatively inexpensive: orchestra tickets cost $1.50 to $2.00 until World War I. But between 1965 and 1969 alone, tickets rose from $6.00 to over $10.00; in 1990, they were $55.00 (Bordman, 723). By the end of the twentieth century, top seats for most productions cost over $100.00, with seats at some of the hottest shows above $500.00.

Inflation has affected the criteria for hit status: shows must now run for longer stretches to be profitable. Thus, while Broadway musicals that ran for more than a few years were comparatively rare in the 1940s, it is now common for musicals to run several years before recouping; conversely, shows running a year or more are often "flops" financially.

As the first resident of the Ford Center for the Performing Arts, for example, the 1998 musical *Ragtime* (music by Stephen Flaherty; book by Terrence McNally; lyrics by Lynn Ahrens) was expected not only to fill the huge stage but also to fill the 1,830-seat auditorium. Marketing for the show was particularly intense, and the spectacle aspect was strongly promoted by producer Garth Drabinsky, under the auspices of his Canadian production company, Livent. Despite relentless publicity and generally positive reviews, the enormously expensive show ran only two years. Although it now boasts a successful life as a regional and international property, *Ragtime* failed to recoup its investment on Broadway, thereby closing as a "flop" in 2000.

The longer average run of Broadway musicals depends in part on an increasingly international audience, which is seen as transitory and ever-renewing. In the prewar era, Broadway served a comparatively local audience; once locals stopped coming, a musical would embark on tour. Yet modern musicals court larger, international audiences by relying on new approaches to spectacle, sophisticated marketing, and more dependence on mass media.

This is especially true since Times Square was renovated in the 1990s. The overhaul of the famously seedy neighborhood began when the city struck a deal with Disney to restore the dilapidated New Amsterdam Theater in exchange for an exclusive lease on the building. This deal attracted other entertainment conglomerates, which have since joined Disney as theater producers.

The presence of such conglomerates has, on the one hand, helped work the American musical back into the web of popular culture from which it was arguably severed in the mid-1950s and, on the other, affected the content of many musicals, a greater number of which rely on familiarity to attract audiences. Thus, there are more revivals on Broadway in recent years, as well as an increase in musicals based on movies or television shows (*The Full Monty*, 2000; *Billy Elliot*, 2008; *Kinky Boots*, 2013; *SpongeBob SquarePants*, 2018).Critics argue that the "corporatization" of musical theater has led to a decline in nuance and a shift toward crass commercialism—as if making money was not an objective on Broadway before 1990. Yet the American musical continues to enjoy enormous populist appeal in its increasingly varied forms. Despite charges that the American musical would fall prey to "corporatization," musicals huge and intimate, innovative and pedestrian, spectacular and simple, on Broadway and on film, in New York and across the country, continue to be developed, performed, and patronized.

SPECTACLE

Aural Spectacle

The term "spectacle" tends to connote the visual, and traditionally relates in some way to human bodies: enormous casts; throngs of leggy chorines in revealing costumes; arrangements of dancers into geometric shapes. Depending on the era and prevailing styles, the visual can range from subtle to spectacular, integrated to irrelevant.

For all its innovation, the 1968 Broadway production of *Hair* (music by Galt MacDermot; book and lyrics by Gerome Ragni and James Rado) was something of a throwback in its approach to visual spectacle. During the act I finale, cast members reenacted a human be-in by dancing naked beneath a huge, flowered sheet. Because the use of full-frontal nudity was a first for Broadway musicals, the scene generated enormous publicity and has since been cited as novel by many critics and historians. But nudity notwithstanding, there was nothing especially groundbreaking about the use of human bodies as a source for visual spectacle.

One innovation with which *Hair* was strongly associated, however—and not always positively—was in its contribution to *aural* spectacle, both in MacDermot's use of rock in the score and in the use of amplification. As purveyors and perpetuators of popular culture, theater composers have always incorporated contemporary sounds into their scores. While *Hair*'s catchy rock score helped earn the production particular acclaim, the musical's reliance on microphones was hardly as celebrated (🎧 Example 8.1).

Amplification has become increasingly common since the advent of rock for several reasons. First, many actors need microphones to protect their voices and to be heard above the electric instruments that accompany them. Second, film and sound recording technologies have exerted significant influence on the stage musical.[6] Third, advances in sound design have allowed theatrical productions to offer cleaner, more balanced sound from the orchestra pit and stage.

Jesus Christ Superstar inadvertently marked an important juncture in this development. When Lloyd Webber and Rice could not get backing for a stage production, they instead recorded an album version, which went gold upon release in 1970.

When Tom O'Horgan's stage version opened on Broadway in 1971, *Superstar* was forced to compete with its own aural predecessor. Despite several frustrating attempts to design a cutting-edge sound system in the Mark Hellinger Theater, O'Horgan and his team could not match the highly polished sound of the extraordinarily successful studio recording. This hurt the production, which—for all its amplification and lavish visual spectacle—struck many spectators as underwhelming when compared with the album (◉ Example 8.2; ◉ Example 8.3).

Though a relatively young field, sound design has become increasingly important since the advent of wireless microphones, computerized mixing boards, and digital sound. Whereas "sound design" was once roughly equivalent to placing microphones around the stage and orchestra pit, sound designers now oversee all sounds—both musical and otherwise—used in a specific production; some even compose and perform the sounds they design. Contemporary stage musicals thus can and often do emulate sound that was once possible only on film.

One recent trend in aural spectacle, however, suggests a retreat from "cinematized" sound. Director John Doyle's revivals of Sondheim's *Sweeney Todd* (2005) and *Company* (2006) departed radically from the original productions. In both revivals, actors all played instruments, and thus the cast provided its own accompaniment. Such productions not only create visual spectacle from what is traditionally perceived aurally but also help remind audiences of the propulsive centrality of a musical's score (◉ Example 8.4).

Visual Spectacle

During the 1970s, visual spectacle took a turn toward the mechanical and electronic, and sets became increasingly elaborate as technology improved. Concerned that elaborate sets were drawing attention from the performers, many critics argued that theater was becoming too cinematic. Yet in spite of jokes about leaving the theater humming the scenery, some of the new sets served their shows beautifully: *Les Misérables*, with its furniture-turned-barricade, rests its complicated story on a set that, while large, is simple and fundamental to the telling of the saga (Example 8.5). *The Lion King* also effectively uses sets and costumes to convey its moods; one might even argue that spectacle lends gravity to this musical's thin plot (Example 8.6).

There are certainly productions that have gone awry despite—or because of—their cinema-sized sets. For example, Lloyd Webber's import *Starlight Express* (1987)—in which trains were embodied by roller-skating actors who zipped around a multitiered hydraulic set that extended above the stage and into the auditorium—failed to charm American audiences (Example 8.7). Similarly, a painstaking rendition of Bay Ridge—complete with miniature subways traversing a network of bridges—could not save the otherwise uninspired 1999 musical version of *Saturday Night Fever*. The set of the Benny Andersson-Björn Ulvaeus-Tim Rice flop *Chess* (1988) is often said to have been so unsightly that it actually deterred audiences.

With *Ragtime*, designer Eugene Lee needed to satisfy a number of challenges: his set had to support the sweeping narrative and simultaneously evoke the simple domesticity of the central characters. The plot of *Ragtime*—based on E. L. Doctorow's 1975 novel—revolves around three families: an upper-middle-class white family in New Rochelle (Mother, Father, and Mother's Little Boy); the Jewish immigrants Tateh and Tateh's Little Girl, who end up on New York's Lower East Side; and the African American family Coalhouse Walker Jr. (a ragtime pianist), Sarah, and their baby. The families and cultures in *Ragtime* clash, often violently, but eventually blend to a degree.

Ragtime has epic breadth, in megamusical fashion, but it also closes in on characters during quiet, reflective moments. The Broadway production balanced large and small, detailed and simple. When Mother gardened, the stage was bare but for a dollhouse-like cut-out of a Victorian home upstage and a row of flowers downstage. Because silhouettes were a recurring theme in the novel, they were incorporated into the show's lyrics and staging: Coalhouse's beloved Model-T Ford is destroyed by racist firemen in silhouette against an orange background (◉ Example 8.8). Other sets were more literal: the nightclub of vaudevillian Evelyn Nesbit (one of several historic figures woven into the story); the Atlantic City boardwalk. Yet during Mother's eleven o'clock number, "Back to Before," the boardwalk melted away, leaving her alone on the stage, thereby allowing the audience to focus entirely on her.

The most effective application of hugeness in *Ragtime* happens when Tateh and his daughter arrive at Ellis Island ("A Shtetl Iz Amereke"; ◉ Example 8.9). Ellis Island is depicted as an enormous gate holding back groups of immigrants, who wave their papers and attempt to surge forward. The gate lifts as they sing, but they move only a few feet before another gate bars their way. This happens several times as they press forward, until the last gate lifts and the immigrants spill across the apron, which has become the Lower East Side. Here, spectacle adds tension and symbolism. *Ragtime*'s design was never invasive or distracting. It was, instead, fluid. The set never inspired its own applause but rather helped convey the mood of each scene.

No amount of sparkle or flash has ever been able to sustain a show that fails to engage an audience emotionally, just as ugly productions tend not to command attention as effectively as those with attractive, appropriate sets. This remains the case regardless of what kind of spectacle is in fashion at any given time. As musicals like *Starlight Express* and *Saturday*

Night Fever demonstrate, overreliance on spectacle is foolish. Nevertheless, the tendency to disparage musicals that incorporate technological innovations simply because they can is unfair. Musical theater has always aimed to entertain audiences aurally *and* visually. As technology continues to change, so will the approach to spectacle.

CHANGING RELATIONSHIPS IN NEW YORK CITY AND BEYOND

The Times Square neighborhood has been home to the greatest concentration of commercial theaters in the country since the turn of the twentieth century. Because the American musical was developed and nurtured on Times Square's many stages, the terms "American musical" and "Broadway musical" are often used interchangeably, even though the musical has become increasingly uprooted from its Broadway pedigree.

Steven Adler writes that Broadway is no longer "an isolated enclave of theatrical activity whose only connection to the rest of the nation [was] as a purveyor of goods. It is now inextricably linked to the network of American theatrical production that barely resembles its earlier incarnation of a few decades past."[7] Indeed, any study that focuses on the American musical as it has developed in the later twentieth century must consider the contributions not only of Off and Off-Off Broadway and the country's many regional theaters, but also a growing number of international concerns.

During the 1960s and 1970s, Off and Off-Off Broadway exerted profound influence on Broadway as an institution. This period was economically and aesthetically difficult for Broadway, but it galvanized the Off Broadway theater scene, which had grown from the Little Theater Movement during the 1950s, and especially the experimental Off-Off Broadway scene, which developed through the 1960s. The Off and Off-Off Broadway realms are responsible for a number of musicals to land on Broadway in recent decades and for several innovative rehearsal and performance techniques.

Hair, for example, had a life in all three theatrical realms, but even in its most famous incarnation on Broadway, it remained very much an Off-Off Broadway baby. *Hair* was written by Gerome Ragni and James Rado, two actors who were affiliated with Joseph Chaikin's experimental Open Theater. While they were performing in Megan Terry's collaborative anti-war piece *Viet Rock* (1966), Ragni and Rado began to document hippies in Greenwich Village. Their notes became a script about the counterculture, which they shopped around town. Producer Joseph Papp chose *Hair* to be the inaugural production of Off Broadway's Public Theater on the condition that Ragni and Rado find a composer to tame their lyrics. Galt MacDermot was hired for the job, and *Hair* opened at the Public for a limited run in 1967. Producer Michael Butler secured rights after the Off Broadway run and set about moving *Hair* to Broadway.

Under the direction of Off-Off Broadway director Tom O'Horgan, the enormously successful Broadway incarnation opened at the Biltmore Theater in 1968. *Hair* was lauded for its contemporary score and gentle depiction of a much-maligned subculture, as well as for its many innovations. In both rehearsal and performance, O'Horgan applied a number of techniques that were common Off-Off Broadway but still novel on Broadway in the late 1960s. These included nontraditional casting; the use of trust and consciousness-raising exercises and collective collaboration in rehearsals; and improvisation, breaks to the fourth wall, performeraudience interaction, and stage nudity in performance.

As a musical that was not cultivated on Broadway, *Hair* is hardly unique. Countless others—including blockbusters like *A Chorus Line, Rent,* and *Spring Awakening*—originated

Off Broadway. In recent years, regional theaters as well have nurtured early versions of productions that eventually reach Broadway.

In the 1980s, during the so-called British Invasion, Broadway became an international business concern as a result of a growing number of "highly capitalised, globally competent and now often transnational players," including British pioneers like composer Andrew Lloyd Webber and producer Cameron Mackintosh (Burston, 206). In 1982, Lloyd Webber imported his musical *Cats*—already a hit in London's West End—to Broadway; the American production also proved enormously successful. Lloyd Webber's earlier Broadway productions—*Jesus Christ Superstar* (1971) and *Evita* (1979), both with lyricist Tim Rice—had garnered plenty of attention, but *Cats* was a cultural phenomenon that made Lloyd Webber a household name.

Thanks in part to intense publicity, *Cats* became an entity known even to those who hadn't seen it. The first of many imported megamusicals, *Cats* ran for twentyone years in the West End and eighteen on Broadway, where it closed in 2002 and 2000, respectively. It has been seen in over twenty countries, and continues to enjoy international success via productions that look remarkably like the original ones.

The idea of musical franchising—in which producers demand that any production hew as closely to the original as possible—is relatively new and strongly associated with the British Invasion. Lloyd Webber, especially when partnered with hands-on producer Cameron Mackintosh, favors the practice. Disappointed by O'Horgan's staging of *Jesus Christ Superstar* in 1971, he sought more control over how his subsequent properties appeared, regardless of where they were staged or who staged them.

Traditionally, when a property is licensed, directors are free to stage the production however they wish. For example, all subsequent productions of *Hair* in the late 1960s and '70s were custom-designed for each city. But with *Cats,* and even more rigidly with Lloyd Webber's *The Phantom of the Opera* and Claude-Michel Schönberg and Alain Boublil's *Les Misérables* (both Mackintosh productions), what one saw in Berlin, Australia, or Japan was identical to what one saw on Broadway.

Theatrical franchising makes sense as a marketing strategy and proves an effective way of generating international exposure: interested audiences do not have to travel to New York or London to see extravagant musicals, and people across the world can experience something they never could before. But the practice has been roundly condemned as "McTheater": a soulless chain of identical productions that destroy local creativity and deprive individual companies of artistic freedom. In response to this criticism, many international properties have held less strictly to foreign staging rules since the 1980s and continue to thrive.

Broadway still serves as the musical theater's symbolic heart, but its grip on the genre has loosened, due to Off and Off-Off Broadway innovations and more recently by the "internationalization" of the musical. The result has allowed for different kinds of musical theater, broader audiences, and the chance for the musical to attain "mass media" status.

ADVERTISING AND MARKETING

Because of the international appeal of the American musical and because of the rising costs of putting on a show, the ways producers have attempted to attract audiences—thus, to sell theater to increasingly broad segments of the world's population—have intensified greatly in recent decades. Since the late 1990s, many new techniques have been applied to the practice of researching and targeting audiences, on both the grassroots and international level. In 1997, *The Audience for New York Theatre*, a landmark study by the company Audience Research and Analysis, was published, sponsored by the League of American Theatres and Producers. Since its appearance, an interest in profiling actual and potential audiences has grown substantially on Broadway and beyond.

Also popular is the practice of synergy, whereupon a company can simultaneously sell a particular product and any number of related products. Synergy allows companies like Disney to rely on familiarity to sell a musical version of, for example, the film *The Little Mermaid*, but also to use the stage version to generate continued interest in the film on DVD and all *Mermaid*-related merchandise. While familiarity has long been used to sell musicals—hence revivals, musicals based on films, and the Tin Pan Alley practice of dropping popular songs into numerous productions—the modern concept of synergy is particularly potent now that entertainment conglomerates are functioning as theater producers.

While the marketing of musicals has become more sophisticated, advertisements have been streamlined and, in some respects, simplified for international audiences. Once franchised musicals began opening in foreign cities, producers began to reinforce the idea that all productions, regardless of setting or language spoken, would be Broadway reproductions. Shows began to be sold like brands: musicals were reduced to simple, striking logos that could appear in the media and on billboards; repetitive musical themes that could saturate radio and television ads; and catchy slogans that would stick in the mind. Mackintosh's early ads for *Cats* teased, "Isn't the curiosity killing you?" The famous logo for the production featured two yellow cat's eyes—the pupils of which are dancing figures—against a black background (▶ Example 8.10). For *Les Misérables*, the equally famous lithograph of young Cosette was adapted for every country (⦿ Example 8.11; ⦿ Example 8.12). *Rent*'s catchy slogan, "No Day But Today," exemplifies the power of simplicity in advertising. The silhouette of a man with upraised arm perched on a star in the *Hamilton* (2015) logo quickly became iconic, representing the rebellious energy of that production. Of course, images and slogans alone do not sell Broadway shows. Producers have also become more reliant on mass media to sell musicals.

Since it was first televised in 1956, the annual Tony Awards ceremony has featured scenes from nominated productions, which help draw audiences to Broadway. Similarly, the occasional talk- or variety-show appearance has boosted sales for many productions; the numbers performed by the cast of *Camelot* on Ed Sullivan's "Toast of the Town" in 1961 resulted in an unprecedented $3.5 million surge in ticket sales. In 1972, the Broadway musical *Pippin* broke new ground by becoming the first Broadway musical featured in a television advertisement.

At present, musicals are advertised on television and radio, before films in movie theaters, and especially via the Internet. Websites like Broadway.com feature extensive theater coverage and allow theatergoers to secure tickets to Broadway shows from anywhere in the world. It is also customary for each Broadway production to have its own website through which tickets can be purchased and production information gleaned; fans, as well, help spread the word via various social media sites. Internet fan sites, on which loyal audience members swap gossip and discuss their favorite shows, also abound; occasionally, as was the case with *The Scarlet Pimpernel*, such sites can support grassroots efforts to keep struggling shows alive.

Mass media have been employed to sell musicals via the reality show. In both the United States and the UK, "American Idol"-style programs have tracked audition processes over the course of a television season. Viewers vote on contestants; the winners earn roles in productions like the West End revival of

The Sound of Music ("How Do You Solve a Problem like Maria?" 2006, UK) and the Broadway revival of *Grease* ("*Grease*: You're the One That I Want!" 2006, United States). And a more recent trend that features beloved musicals staged live on television revives a 1950s approach with a contemporary twist: home-viewers are encouraged to connect with others via social media by tweeting their reactions to every scene, performer, and musical number.

Because producers have always been invested in appealing to as many potential spectators as possible, marketing techniques may be more sophisticated, but the philosophy behind them is not new. As with the approach to spectacle, approaches to advertising and marketing have intensified, but only as the technology has allowed and the business of production has demanded.

NOSTALGIA AND REVISIONISM IN THE POSTMODERN AGE

John Bush Jones notes that the precondition for widespread nostalgia—a collective desire to return to a "younger, more innocent, less jaded" time—is "severe discontent with the present" (Jones, 305–6). Musicals have long relied on emotional pull to connect with audiences, but nostalgia has an especially strong impact during or immediately after periods of national hardship. Certainly Rodgers and Hammerstein understood nostalgia's pull: *South Pacific* (1949) allowed American audiences to relive "the Good War"—and perhaps to reinvent it as less personally disruptive, frightening, or tragic—shortly after its resolution.

One of the most successful examples of nostalgia in the musical theater is *Grease* (1972), which capitalized on the '50s craze that developed in America in the early 1970s and lasted through much of that turbulent decade. A light romp through an era that was collectively idealized as relatively safe and innocent (if also socially conformist and politically conservative), *Grease* became the longest-running musical in Broadway history for its time. Audiences continue to embrace this idealized take on '50s teen culture, which was made into a successful film in 1978 and has been revived on Broadway twice: in 1994 and after the 2006 reality series discussed above.

Other postwar musicals that evoke nostalgic affection for their times include *Annie* (1977), *42nd Street* (1980), *Dreamgirls* (1981), *Little Shop of Horrors* (1982), *Miss Saigon* (1991), *Crazy For You* (1992), *The Who's Tommy* (1993), *Mamma Mia!* (2001), *Hairspray* (2002), and *The Drowsy Chaperone* (2006). These shows—and countless others—vary in the degree to which they draw on period-appropriate musical styles. But the sounds of the past trigger nostalgia, and thus an emotional connection. This is the driving logic behind the jukebox musical, a subgenre that has, as noted above, become ubiquitous since the turn of the twenty-first century. New musicals, not based on known sources or repertoire, can evoke nostalgia too; *Hamilton* draws on the audience's perceived notion of an idealized, optimistic young America to create a sense of patriotic familiarity.

Instead of offering new songs evocative of past styles, jukebox musicals string together preexisting songs by a popular artist or group with the aid of a unifying (often frivolous) plot. Audiences of jukebox musicals tend to enter the theater familiar not only with the era but also with the songs themselves. As a result, the lure of familiarity is strong, gasps of recognition are frequent, and singing along during performances is common.

Jukebox musicals have clear precedents in film but are also influenced by shows like Tom O'Horgan's *Sgt. Pepper's Lonely Hearts Club Band on the Road* (1974) and the faux-concert

Beatlemania (1977). The jukebox musical's own golden age began, perhaps unsurprisingly, after 2001, during a period of monumental uncertainty that caused a surge of collective nostalgia. Jukebox musicals that have opened since 2001 to varying degrees of success include *Mamma Mia!* (2001), *Movin' Out* (2002), *Jersey Boys* (2005), *All Shook Up* (2005), *Rock of Ages* (2009), *Million Dollar Quartet* (2010), *Motown the Musical* (2013), *Beautiful: The Carole King Musical* (2013) and *On Your Feet!* (2015).

Some productions present a much subtler brand of nostalgia. *Ragtime*, for example, does not play on the audience's experience with an era but instead with the characters' experiences of their own past. While the Doctorow book is told by an omniscient narrator, the characters narrate their own lives in the stage version, in past tense and the third person, as if they are experiencing events and reflecting on them simultaneously: "The house on the hill in New Rochelle was Mother's domain," Mother announces in the prologue. "She took pleasure in making it comfortable for the men of her family."[8] The many historical figures (Evelyn Nesbit, Booker T. Washington, Harry Houdini, Emma Goldman, Henry Ford, J. P. Morgan) whose stories are woven into the musical introduce themselves similarly: "Evelyn Nesbit was the most beautiful woman in America." This narrative affectation frames the show: the audience watches the characters watch their own pasts, some from beyond the grave.

Flaherty's score refers to a variety of genres, most of which are rooted in turn-of-the-century styles: ragtime, the blues, the parlor waltz. Although there is a fair amount of belting, the general color of the score is bittersweet, gentle. *Grease*, like many jukebox musicals, features a score that is almost consistently upbeat; the audience generates its own nostalgia for the sound (🅐 Example 8.13). Yet in *Ragtime,* fondness and a sweet sense of loss are built into the score. Consider, for example, Mother and Tateh's tentative meeting in "Nothing Like the City," or the preordained doom of Mother's Younger Brother in "He Wanted to Say" (🔊 Example 8.14; 🔊 Example 8.15). The music, like the action, is simultaneously nostalgic and present.

As with other musicals that play on a less immediate sense of nostalgia—*Fiddler on the Roof* (1964), for example—the events depicted in *Ragtime* are often violent and upsetting, but distance keeps us safe. Ultimately, musicals like *Grease* and *Ragtime* function similarly, despite different approaches: both allow audiences to long for an idealized past, but perhaps to be simultaneously thankful that the past is gone.

Nostalgia applies not only to musicals themselves but also to the legacy of many composers who have created them. The musical theater has its own canon, which is reflected in the constant flow of revivals that appear on Broadway stages. And nostalgia has colored the individual careers of, for example, Stephen Sondheim, who has earned the reputation among many critics and historians as the sole remaining representative of the mythic, storied past.

Sondheim has not enjoyed the international success experienced by some of his contemporaries. Most of his musicals are intimate in comparison with, for example, megamusicals or Disney spectacles. Both musically and dramaturgically, Sondheim's works tend to be denser and darker and are thus often perceived as less accessible. Because his musicals don't tend to translate to international audiences, they are not marketed aggressively to them.

What is misleading about Sondheim's placement in the musical theater canon is that while he was strongly influenced by the songwriting teams of the so-called Golden Age—in particular, Richard Rodgers and Oscar Hammerstein II—his sound is hardly rooted in the past; nor is he the last living practitioner of the sort of "authentic" musical that purportedly died when the Golden Age passed. Sondheim has always embraced bold, experimental, and contemporary sounds (● Example 8.16). The many young composers Sondheim has influenced—Jason Robert Brown, Adam Guettel, Jonathan Larson, and Jeanine Tesori, for example—have all clearly absorbed myriad musical influences that are reflected in their scores.

The fact that nostalgia involves collective revisionism is enormously important when it comes to the examination of contemporary musicals. The American musical is often seen to reflect American culture, but to some degree, the form simultaneously reinvents culture as well. Musicals depend on a collective—but also a *selective*—interest in the past. Thus, more work needs to be done on how musicals of the past fifty years have negotiated contemporary cultural demons: AIDS (*Falsettos, Rent*); race and class (*In the Heights, Passing Strange, Caroline, or Change*); sexuality and gender (*Hedwig and the Angry Inch, Wicked, Spring Awakening*; ● Example 8.17). Also relevant here are the ways older musicals are revisited. For example, the 1999 revival of Irving Berlin's *Annie Get Your Gun* (1946) altered several scenes seen as offensive to Native Americans, sparking debate about whether classic shows should be changed to fit contemporary sensibilities.

Scholars must keep in mind that not only nostalgia but also cultural memory can be selectively fabricated. Composers of musicals comment selectively on racial, sexual, economic, political, and sociocultural ups and downs. They have also begun to comment, often with great insight, on the musical's own history: a slew of self-referential, postmodern musicals, including *Bat Boy: The Musical* (2001), *The Producers* (2001), *Avenue Q* (2003), *[title of show]* (2004), *Monty Python's Spamalot* (2005), and *Something Rotten!* (2015) look back on their own legacy with affection and witty insight (● Example 8.18). In exploring the sociocultural relevance of contemporary musicals, the scholar must tease out what is cultural reflection and what is cultural revision.

CONCLUSIONS

Although set in the past and infused with nostalgia, *Ragtime* is a modern musical: it had huge (although not always complicated) sets, employed unusual narrative techniques, featured a pastiche of musical styles, relied on massive publicity, and while financially unsuccessful on Broadway, still achieved international success. The musical does not necessarily align itself with any previous or current tradition, except in the broadest of strokes: it was influenced by a century of tradition but also contains innovations and surprises. Yet in commenting on contemporary productions, many critics and scholars resort to comparisons with the past. In his review of *Ragtime* for the *Village Voice* (February 3, 1998), Michael Feingold evokes the Golden Age (he locates it between "the century's teens" and the early 1960s) in arguing that the musical—that "very unhappy art form"—is stuck in a "silver age." Feingold liked *Ragtime* but felt it lacked "the extra lighthearted spark that made the old musicals great." He mournfully concludes that "here and now, this is the best we can do."

It is our hope that the tendency toward simplistic comparisons of the "golden" past with the tarnished present will fall away as musical scholarship becomes more varied and sophisticated. Musicals are not what they were: time has elapsed; technology, economics, politics, and culture have shifted. Yet while perhaps not as central to popular culture as before, musicals have not stopped being relevant or influential, just as their audiences have not gotten stupider, lazier, or less emotionally connected. Contemporary musical theater draws from the past while simultaneously offering modern innovations. We scholars must continue to do the same.

NOTES

1. See, for example, Geoffrey Block, *Enchanted Evenings: The Broadway Musical from* Show Boat *to* Sondheim (New York: Oxford University Press, 1997), Gerald Bordman, *American Musical Theatre: A Chronicle*, 3rd ed. (New York: Oxford University Press, 2001), *The Cambridge Companion to the Musical*, 2nd ed., ed. William A. Everett, and Paul R. Laird (Cambridge: Cambridge University Press, 2008), Denny Martin Flinn, *Musical! A Grand Tour: The Rise, Glory, and Fall of an American Institution* (New York: Schirmer, 1997), Mark. N. Grant, *The Rise and Fall of the Broadway Musical* (Hanover, NH: University Press of New England, 2004), Gerald Mast, *Can't Help Singin': The American Musical on Stage and Screen* (New York: Overlook Press, 1987), and Ethan Mordden, *The Happiest Corpse I've Ever Seen: The Last 25 Years of the Broadway Musical* (New York: Palgrave Macmillan, 2004).
2. Allen Woll, *Black Musical Theatre from* Coontown *to* Dreamgirls (New York: Da Capo, 1989), p. 248.
3. Mordden, for example, regularly makes assumptions about contemporary audiences and their inability to appreciate musicals that he has deemed "sophisticated."
4. Bordman also includes Cy Coleman, Charles Strouse, and "possibly Jerry Herman" in his list of post-1960s composers "willing or able" to supply the theater with memorable scores (721).
5. John Bush Jones, *Our Musicals, Ourselves: A Social History of the American Musical Theatre* (Hanover, NH: University Press of New England, 2003), p. 83.
6. See Jonathan Burston, "Theatre Space as Virtual Place: Audio Technology, the Reconfigured Singing Body, and the Megamusical" (*Popular Music* 17.2 [May 1998]: 205–18).
7. Steven Adler, *On Broadway: Art and Commerce on the Great White Way* (Carbondale: Southern Illinois University Press, 2004, p. 4.
8. This and all other quotations from *Ragtime*: Lynn Ahrens, Stephen Flaherty, and Terrence McNally, libretto (Original Broadway Cast Recording, BMG Entertainment, 1998).

REFERENCES

References for Volume I, Introduction

Dyer, Richard. "Entertainment and Utopia." In *Genre: The Musical*. Edited by Rick Altman. London: Routledge and Kegan Paul, 1981; originally published in *Movie* 2 (Spring 1977), 2–13.

McMillin, Scott. *The Musical as Drama: A Study of the Principles and Conventions behind Musical Shows from Kern to Sondheim*. Princeton: Princeton University Press, 2006.

Miranda, Lin-Manuel. "Stephen Sondheim, Theater's Greatest Lyricist." *New York Times*, October 16, 2017. https://www.nytimes.com/2017/10/16/t-magazine/lin-manuel-miranda-stephen-sondheim.html?_r=0 Accessed November 25, 2017.

Wolf, Stacy. "In Defense of Pleasure: Musical Theatre History in the Liberal Arts [A Manifesto]." *Theatre Topics* 17.1 (March 2007): 51–60.

References for Volume I, Chapter 1

Butterfield, Herbert. *The Whig Interpretation of History*. London: G. Bell & Sons, 1931.

Frye, Northrop. "Literary History." *New Literary History* 12.2 (Winter 1981): 219–25.

Goehr, Lydia. *The Imaginary Museum of Musical Works: An Essay in the Philosophy of Music*. Oxford: Oxford University Press, 1992.

Hickey, Dave. "Buying the World." *Daedalus* 131.4 (Fall, 2002): 69–87.

Iggers, Georg G. *Historiography in the Twentieth Century: From Scientific Objectivity to the Postmodern Challenge. With a New Epilogue*. Middletown, CT: Wesleyan University, Press, 2005.

Kerman, Joseph. *Opera as Drama, New and Revised Edition*. Berkeley: University of California Press, 1988.

Stone, Lawrence. "The Revival of Narrative: Reflections on a New Old History." *Past & Present* (November 1979): 3–24.

Treitler, Leo. "The Present as History." *Perspectives of New Music* 7.2 (Spring–Summer 1969): 1–58.

Weber, William. "Beyond Zeitgeist: Recent Work in Music History." *Journal of Modern History* 66/2 (June 1994): 321–25.

White, Hayden. *Metahistory: The Historical Imagination in Nineteenth-Century Europe*. Baltimore: Johns Hopkins University Press, 1973.

References for Volume I, Chapter 2

Banfield, Stephen. *Sondheim's Broadway Musicals*. Ann Arbor: University of Michigan Press, 1993.

Barthes, Roland. *Image, Music, Text*. Ed. and trans. Stephen Heath. New York: Hill and Wang, 1977.

Beckerman, Bernard. *Theatrical Presentation: Performer, Audience, and Act*. London: Routledge, 1990.

Decker, Todd. "'Do You Want to Hear a Mammy Song?' A Historiography of *Show Boat*." *Contemporary Theatre Review* 19.1 (2009): 8–21.

———. Show Boat: *Performing Race in an American Musical*. Oxford and New York: Oxford University Press, 2013.

Eagleton, Terry. *Literary Theory: An Introduction*. 2nd edition. Minneapolis: University of Minnesota Press, 1996.

Elam, Kier. *The Semiotics of Theatre and Drama*. 2nd ed. London: Routledge, 2002.

Foucault, Michel. "What Is an Author?" In *Textual Strategies: Perspectives in Post-Structuralist Criticism*. Edited and translated by Josué V. Harari. Ithaca, NY: Cornell University Press, 1979, 141–60.

Honzl, Jindřich. "Dynamics in the Sign in the Theater." In *Semiotics of Art: Prague School Contributions*. Edited by L. Matejka and K. Pomorsak. Cambridge, MA: MIT Press, 1976, 74–93.

Iser, Wolfgang. *The Act of Reading: A Theory of Aesthetic Response.* Baltimore: Johns Hopkins University Press, 1980.

Kirle, Bruce. *Unfinished Show Business: Broadway Musicals as Works-in-Process.* Carbondale: Southern Illinois University Press, 2005.

Knapp, Raymond. *The American Musical and the Formation of National Identity.* Princeton, NJ: Princeton University Press, 2005.

Kreuger, Miles. *Show Boat: The Story of a Classic American Musical.* New York: Da Capo Press, 1977.

McMillin, Scott. "Paul Robeson, Will Vodery's 'Jubilee Singers,' and the Earliest Script of the Kern-Hammerstein *Show Boat.*" *Theatre Survey* 41 (2000): 51–70.

——— *The Musical as Drama: A Study of the Principles and Conventions behind Musical Shows from Kern to Sondheim.* Princeton, NJ: Princeton University Press, 2006.

Radloff, Bernard. "Text." In *Encyclopedia of Contemporary Literary Theory: Approaches, Scholars, Terms.* Edited by Irena R. Makaryk. Toronto: University of Toronto Press, 1993, 639–41.

Rodgers, Richard. *Musical Stages: An Autobiography.* New York: Random House, 1975.

Pfister, Manfred. *The Theory and Analysis of Drama.* Translated by John Halliday. Cambridge: Cambridge University Press, 1988.

Sartre, Jean-Paul. *What Is Literature?* Translated by Bernard Frechtman. London: Routledge, 2001.

Savran, David. "Toward a Historiography of the Popular." *Theatre Survey* 45.2 (November 2004): 211–17.

Swain, Joseph P. *The Broadway Musical; A Critical and Musical Survey,* 2nd edition. Lanham, MD: Scarecrow Press, 2002.

Taruskin, Richard. *Text and Act: Essays on Music and Performance.* New York: Oxford University Press, 1995.

References for Volume I, Chapter 3

Bergeen, Laurence. *As Thousands Cheer: The Life of Irving Berlin.* New York: Viking, 1990.

Engel, Lehmann. *American Musical Theater.* New York: Macmillan, 1975.

Gottlieb, Jack. *Funny, It Doesn't Sound Jewish: How Yiddish Songs and Synagogue Melodies Influenced Tin Pan Alley, Broadway, and Hollywood.* Albany: State University of New York in association with the Library of Congress, 2004.

Knapp, Raymond. *The American Musical and the Formation of National Identity.* Princeton, NJ: Princeton University Press, 2005.

——. "'How great thy charm, thy sway how excellent!' Tracing Gilbert and Sullivan's Legacy in the American Musical," *The Cambridge Companion to Gilbert and Sullivan.* Ed. David Eden and Meinhard Saremba. Cambridge: Cambridge University Press, 2009, pp. 201–15.

Knowles, Mark. *Tap Roots: The Early History of Tap Dancing.* Jefferson, NC: McFarland, 2002.

Laird, Paul R. *The Musical Theater of Stephen Schwartz: From Godspell to Wicked and Beyond.* Lanham, MD: Rowman and Littlefield, 2014.

Most, Andrea. *Making Americans: Jews and the Broadway Musical.* Cambridge, MA: Harvard University Press, 2004.

References for Volume I, Chapter 4

Anderson, John Murray. *Out without My Rubbers.* New York: Library Publishers, 1954.

Barker, Barbara. Unprocessed papers. Box 18, box 5, box 6. Research materials of Agnes de Mille, New York Public Library for the Performing Arts, Dance Division, New York, NY.

Beiswanger, George. "New Images in Dance: Martha Graham and Agnes de Mille" *Theatre Arts* 28.10 (October 1944): 609–14

De Mille, Agnes. *Martha.* New York: Random House, 1991.

Evans, Harvey. Interview by Liza Gennaro. March 3, 2003 transcript. Oral History Collection, Lincoln Center Library of the Performing Arts, New York.

Gelb, Arthur. "Robbins and His 'Courage.'" *New York Times* (April 28, 1963): 127.

Gilvey, John Anthony. *Before the Parade Passes By: Gower Champion and the Glorious American Musical.* New York: St. Martin's Press, 2005.

Gottschild, Brenda Dixon. *Digging the African American Presence in American Performance.* Westport, CT: Praeger, 1996.

Hardy, Camille. Popular Balanchine Dossiers 1927–2004. *"Boys from Syracuse."* Box 15. New York Public Library for the Performing Arts, Dance Division, New York, NY.

Hill, Constance Valis. "From Bharata Natyam to Bop: Jack Cole's 'Modern' Jazz Dance." *Dance Research Journal* 33.2 (Winter 2001–2): 29–39.

———. Popular Balanchine Dossiers 1927–2004. *"Babes in Arms."* Box 14. New York Public Library for the Performing Arts, Dance Division, New York, NY. 2002.

Horst, Louis. *Modern Dance Forms and Its Relation to the Other Modern Arts.* New York: Dance Horizons, 1961.

Ingber, Judith Brin. "Dancing into Marriage." *Arabesque* 7.4 (1982): 8–9, 20–21.

Johnson, Harriet. "The First Steps in a Robbins Dance: It's Planning Says *Billion Dollar Baby* Choreographer." *New York Post*, January 4, 1946.

Jones, Bill T. Telephone interview with Liza Gennaro. May 18, 2007.

Jowitt, Deborah. *Jerome Robbins: His Life, His Theater, His Dance.* New York: Simon & Schuster, 2004.

Keller, Kate Van Winkle, and Charles Cyril Hendrickson. *George Washington: A Biography in Social Dance.* Sandy Hook, CT: Hendrickson Group, 1998.

Kislan, Richard. *Hoofing on Broadway: A History of Show Dancing.* New York: Prentice Hall, 1986.

Lawrence, Greg. *Dance with Demons: The Life of Jerome Robbins.* New York: Berkley Books, 2001.

Loney, Glenn. *Unsung Genius: The Passion of Dancer-Choreographer Jack Cole.* New York: Franklin Watts, 1984.

Malone, Jacqui. *Steppin' on the Blues: The Visual Rhythms of African American Dance.* Urbana: University of Illinois Press, 1996.

Martin, Ethel. Interview by Liza Gennaro. February 26, 2003 transcript. Oral History Collection, Lincoln Center Library of the Performing Arts, New York.

Ries, Frank W.D. "Albertine Rasch: The Broadway Career." *Dance Chronical* 6:2 (1983): 95–137.

Shimer, Genevieve, and Kate van Winkle. *The Playford Ball: 103 Early Country Dances*. Chicago: A Cappella Books and the Country Dance and Song Society, 1990.

Stearns, Marshall and Jean. *Jazz Dance*. New York: Macmillan, 1968.

Stratyner, Barbara. *Ned Wayburn and the Dance Routine: From Vaudeville to the Ziegfeld Follies*. *Studies in Dance History* No. 13. Madison: University of Wisconsin Press for the Society of Dance Scholars, 1996.

Vaill, Amanda. *Somewhere: The Life of Jerome Robbins*. New York: Broadway Books, 2006.

Wayburn, Ned. *The Art of Stage Dancing: The Story of a Beautiful and Profitable Profession*. New York: Belvedere, 1980.

References for Volume I, Chapter 5

Bogle, Donald. *Toms, Coons, Mulattoes, Mammies, and Bucks: An Interpretive History of Blacks in American Films*. 4th ed. New York: Continuum, 2001.

Cockrell, Dale. *Demons of Disorder: Early Blackface Minstrels and Their World*. Cambridge: Cambridge UP, 1997.

Krasner, David. *Resistance, Parody and Double Consciousness in African American Theatre, 1895–1910*. New York: St. Martin's Press, 1997.

Llamon, W. T. Jr. *Raising Cain: Blackface Performance from Jim Crow to Hip Hop*. Cambridge, MA: Harvard UP, 1998.

Lott, Eric. *Love and Theft: Blackface Minstrelsy and American Working Class*. New York: Oxford UP, 1993.

Mahar, William J. *Behind the Burnt Cork Mask: Early Blackface Minstrelsy and Antebellum American Popular Culture*. Urbana: University of Illinois Press, 1999.

McAllister, Marvin. *White People Do Not Know How to Behave at Entertainments Designed for Ladies and Gentlemen of Colour*. Chapel Hill: University of North Carolina Press, 2003.

Riis, Thomas. *American Minstrel Music*. Oxford Bibliographies Online, 2016.

Rourke, Constance. *American Humor: A Study of the National Character*. Garden City, NY: Doubleday, 1953; originally published 1931.

Simond, Ike. *Old Slack's Reminiscence and Pocket History of the Colored Profession from 1865 to 1891*. Reprint edition. Popular Press: Bowling Green, OH, 1974; originally published 1891.

References for Volume I, Chapter 6

Bordman, Gerald. *American Musical Theatre: A Chronicle*. 3rd ed. New York: Oxford University Press, 2001.

Decker, Todd. *Show Boat: Performing Race in an American Musical*. Oxford and New York: Oxford University Press, 2013.

Furia, Philip. *The Poets of Tin Pan Alley: A History of America's Great Lyricists*. New York: Oxford University Press, 1990.

"Internet Broadway Database." http://www.ibdb.com.

Knapp, Raymond. *The American Musical and the Formation of National Identity*. Princeton, NJ: Princeton University Press, 2005.

———. *The American Musical and the Performance of Personal Identity*. Princeton, NJ: Princeton University Press, 2006.

Randel, Don M., Matthew Shaftel, and Susan Forscher Weiss, eds. *A Cole Porter Companion*. University of Illinois Press, 2016.

Riis, Jacob A. *How the Other Half Lives: Studies among the Tenements of New York*. New York, 1890. Rep. New York: Kessinger Publishers, 2004. Online at www.authentichistory.com/1865-1897/progressive/riis/index.html.

Subotnik, Rose Rosengard. "Shoddy Equipment for Living? Deconstructing the Tin Pan Alley Song." *Musicological Identities: Essays in Honor of Susan McClary*. Ed. Steven Baur, Raymond Knapp, and Jacqueline Warwick. Aldershot, UK: Ashgate, 2008, pp. 205–18.

Further Reading for Volume I, Chapter 7

Block, Geoffrey. "The Broadway Canon from *Show Boat* to *West Side Story* and the European Operatic Ideal." *Journal of Musicology* 11.4 (Fall 1993): 525–44.

Block, Geoffrey. *Enchanted Evenings: The Broadway Musical from "Show Boat" to Sondheim and Lloyd Webber*. New York: Oxford University Press, 1997; 2nd ed., 2009.

Hammerstein, Oscar II. "In Re 'Oklahoma!': The adaptor-Lyricist Describes How the Musical Hit Came Into Being." *New York Times*, May 23, 1943, p. 11.

Hammerstein, Oscar II. "Notes on Lyrics." *Lyrics*. Milwaukee: Hal Leonard Books, 1985.

McMillin, Scott. *The Musical as Drama: A Study of the Principles and Conventions behind Musical Shows from Kern to Sondheim*. Princeton, NJ: Princeton University Press, 2006.

Mueller, John. "Fred Astaire and the Integrated Musical." *Cinema Journal* 24.1 (Fall 1984): 28–40.

Prince, Hal. *Contradictions: Notes on Twenty-six Years in the Theatre*. New York: Dodd, Mead, 1974.

Reid, Louis R. "Composing While You Wait." *The Dramatic Mirror*, June 2, 1917: 5.

Rodgers, Richard. *Musical Stages: An Autobiography*. New York: Random House, 1975; repr. New York: Da Capo, 1995, 2000.

Swain, Joseph P. *The Broadway Musical: A Critical and Musical Survey*. Oxford: Oxford University Press, 1990; 2nd ed., Lanham, MD: Scarecrow Press, 2002.

Further Reading for Volume I, Chapter 8

Adler, Steven. *On Broadway: Art and Commerce on the Great White Way*. Carbondale: Southern Illinois University Press, 2004.

Burston, Jonathan. "Theatre Space as Virtual Place: Audio Technology, the Reconfigured Singing Body, and the Megamusical." *Popular Music* 17.2 (May 1998): 205–18.

Everett, William A. and Paul R. Laird, eds. *The Cambridge Companion to the Musical*, 2nd ed. Cambridge: Cambridge University Press, 2008.

Jones, John Bush. *Our Musicals, Ourselves: A Social History of the American Musical Theatre*. Hanover, NH: University Press of New England, 2003.

Sternfeld, Jessica. *The Megamusical*. Indiana University Press, 2006.

Sternfeld, Jessica and Elizabeth L. Wollman, eds. *The Routledge Companion to the Contemporary American Stage Musical*. New York: Routledge, 2018.

Wollman, Elizabeth L. *A Critical Companion to the American Stage Musical*. New York and London: Bloomsbury, 2017.

Wollman, Elizabeth L. *Hard Times: The Adult Musical in 1970s New York City*. New York: Oxford University Press, 2013.

Wollman, Elizabeth L. *The Theater Will Rock: A History of the Rock Musical from* Hair *to* Hedwig. Ann Arbor, Mich.: University of Michigan Press, 2006.

INDEX

Note: Page numbers in *italics* indicate photographs.

"The Death of the Author"
(Barthes), 39
Decker, Todd, 43
"Deep into the Ground," 58
Deitz, Howard, 78
De Koven, Reginald, 64
de Mille, Agnes: and attribution
issues, 14; choreography style
of, 78–80, 87, 91–93; and
concept musicals, 165; and
Fosse's style, 88–90; influence
on later choreographers, 84;
and integration of musicals,
154, 161–63; and *Oklahoma!*,
44, 72; and "open text" view of
musicals, 38–39
The Desert Song, 54
Destry Rides Again, 88
dialect songs, 110
dialogue, 156
Dibdin, Charles, 103
Die Fledermaus, 65
directors. *See also specific individuals*
Disney, 190
Dixon, George Washington, 109
Doctorow, E. L., 184
Don't Bother Me, I Can't Cope, 61
Do the Right Thing, 121
Doyle, John, 183
Drabinsky, Garth, 180
Dramatist Guild, 84
Dreamgirls, 91; and integration of
musicals, 167; and nostalgia, 193
The Drowsy Chaperone, 67, 193
Du Bois, W. E. B., 153
Dyer, Richard, 1

Eagleton, Terry, 35, 39
Early Music movement, 36
"Easy to Be Hard," 60
economics of musical
productions, 178–81

"Edelweiss," 57
Edge of the City, 121
Elam, Kier, 30, 32–35
"El Capitan," 64
"eleven o'clock numbers," 53
Ellington, Duke, 56
Elssler, Fanny, 114
"Embraceable You," 66
Emmett, Dan, 100, 109
*Encyclopedia of Contemporary
Literary Theory* (Radloff), 32
Engel, Lehman, 52–53, 66–68
Erie Canal, 104
Ethiopian Serenaders, 110, *111*
ethnicity, 127–35, 148–49n4. *See
also* race issues and racism
European influences, 188–89
Evita, 188
expressive modes, 35–36

Face the Music, 160
Fancy Free, 80, 95n21
fans and fan practice.
See audiences
"The Farmer and the Cowman," 156
"Fascinating Rhythm," 56, 143–44
Feingold, Michael, 197
Felix, Seymour, 75
"Female American Serenaders," 114
femininity and feminism. *See*
gender and sexuality
Fiddler on the Roof: and
attribution issues, 37–38;
and choreography, 83, 90;
and concept musicals, 165–
67; and the Golden Age of
musicals, 72; and integration
of musicals, 172; and musical
styles, 59; and nostalgia, 195;
and race/ethnicity issues, 59
Fields, W. C., 119
Fierstein, Harvey, 37

Jews and Jewish
Americans, 59
"Jim Crow" (act), 108–9
John, Elton, 41, 61–62
Johnny Johnson, 160
Johnson, Billy, 117
Johnson, Harriet, 81
Johnson, J. Rosamund, 137
Johnson, Lew, 113
joke songs, 68–69
The Jolly Bachelors, 129–31
Jolson, Al, 120
Jones, Bill T., 92
Jones, John Bush, 192
Jonson, Ben, 103
Joplin, Scott, 54
*Joseph and the Amazing Technicolor
Dreamcoat,* 66, 68
Joyce, James, 145
Jubilee, 59
Judgment of Paris, 90
jukebox musicals, 62, 193–94
Jullien, Louis, 112
Jungle Fever, 121

"Kansas City," 156
Kaufman, George S., 161, 165
Keeler, Ruby, 67
Keller, Kate Van Winkle, 87
Kelly, Emmett, 117
Kelly, Gene, 67
Kerman, Joseph, 22, 30
Kern, Jerome: and attribution
issues, 42–43, 46; and dance
styles, 75–76; and the Golden
Age of musicals, 177; and
integration of musicals,
153–54, 158–59, 161–62, 170;
and musical styles, 57; and Tin
Pan Alley, 136, 139
Kidd, Michael, 84, 88

King, Carole, 61
The King and I: and dance/
choreography, 81–82; and
dance styles, 65
"King Herod's Song," 60
"The King's Barcarolle," 65
Kinky Boots, 181
Kirle, Bruce, 34–37
Kismet, 86–87
Kiss Me, Kate, 143, 172–73
klezmer music, 59
Knapp, Raymond, 30, 159–60
Knipp, Chuck, 122
Kolodin, Irving, 87
Krafft–Ebing, Richard
von, 150n19
Kreuger, Miles, 43–45

Lady, Be Good, 56, 143
Lady in the Dark, 47, 162
"Land of the Gay
Caballero," 59
Lapine, James, 164
Larson, Jonathan, 62, 196
Latessa, Dick, 37
Latin ethnicity and culture,
58–59, 90
Laurents, Arthur: and concept
musicals, 165; and *West Side
Story,* 84
"Laurey Makes Up Her Mind"
(dance), 156, 161
Lawrence, Gertrude, 47
Lee, Eugene, 184
Lee, Gypsy Rose, 83
Lee, Sammy, 75–76
Lee, Spike, 121
Lehár, Franz, 64, 157
Leon, Francis, 114
Leonard, Eddie, *118*
Lerner, Alan Jay, 65, 67–68, 166